COMPASSIONATE JESUS

COMPASSIONATE JESUS

Rethinking the Christian's Approach to Modern Medicine

Christopher Bogosh

Reformation Heritage Books
Grand Rapids, Michigan

Reformation Heritage Books
2965 Leonard St. NE
Grand Rapids, MI 49525
616-977-0889 / Fax 616-285-3246
orders@heritagebooks.org
www.heritagebooks.org

Printed in the United States of America
13 14 15 16 17 18/10 9 8 7 6 5 4 3 2 1

Library of Congress Cataloging-in-Publication Data

Bogosh, Christopher W.
  Compassionate Jesus : rethinking the Christian's approach to modern medicine / Christopher W. Bogosh.
      pages cm
  ISBN 978-1-60178-228-1 (pbk. : alk. paper) 1. Medicine—Religious aspects—Christianity. I. Title.
  BT732.2.B64 2013
  261.5'61—dc23
                          2013011093

For additional Reformed literature, request a free book list from Reformation Heritage Books at the above regular or e-mail address.

To

Jesus

"The author and finisher of our faith,
who for the joy that was set before Him
endured the cross, despising the shame,
and has sat down at the right hand
of the throne of God."

—Hebrews 12:2

Contents

Acknowledgments

I heard Rev. Dr. Joel Beeke preach for the first time at the Bolton Conference in Upton, Massachusetts, in the autumn of 2003. His sermon on the contrast between Mt. Sinai and Mt. Zion from Hebrews 12:18–24 was a firestorm to my soul. I literally trembled in my seat and wept over my sins as the terror of Mt. Sinai laid heavy upon me, but then Joel brought me to Mt. Zion and "to Jesus the Mediator of the new covenant." My heart fluttered, and my weeping turned to joy! I recall this *experiential* story for a couple reasons. First, Dr. Beeke's Spirit-blessed ministry has cultivated in me a longing to be, in his words, a "sin hater, Christ lover, and holiness pursuer," and, second, I am amazed at how the Spirit has blessed his work since 2003 (a mere ten years ago) at the Puritan Reformed Theological Seminary and Reformation Heritage Books (RHB). I am grateful for Joel's dedication and powerful witness to the Lord Jesus Christ, the transformative effect his ministry has had on my life through his teaching on experiential Calvinism, and for his willingness to publish *Compassionate Jesus* to advance the kingdom of God in the complex world of modern medicine.

Of course, serving alongside Joel is the team of dedicated, Christ-loving RHB staff members who made this book possible. Jay Collier works diligently behind the scenes on so many books at RHB; I am thankful for his philosophical and theological insights and for suggesting ways to make this book more accessible to the lay reader. I am so very, very, grateful for Annette Gysen. Her expert editorial work made this book clearer, and her queries helped me think more deeply about sensitive issues raised throughout *Compassionate Jesus*. There are some wonderful epitaphs on gravestones from the time of Puritan New England, and I think this one dedicated to the wife of a deacon fits Annette well: "She is a godly ornament of the Christian faith." Thanks to all at RHB for their willingness to take up and invest in this out-of-character project!

I am grateful for Dr. Anthony Van Grouw. His medical expertise, advice, and input were very helpful.

Last, but not least, I am grateful for the people I had the opportunity to minister to (a few of whom are mentioned in this book), my colleagues, my family, and my brothers and sisters in Christ. Most of all, I am overwhelmingly grateful to Him to whom this book is dedicated—Jesus.

Introduction

Frank, a middle-aged man, lay on the table in the cold electrophysiology lab.[1] Two weeks earlier Frank had died from a cardiac arrest due to an abnormal heartbeat (lethal heart dysrhythmia), but state-of-the-art medical care and an external cardiac defibrillator, a device that shocks the heart to restore a normal heartbeat, had brought him back to life. As a result, Frank had an automatic implantable cardiac defibrillator (AICD) placed in his body. When Frank's heart fibrillated, it quivered because of electronic disorganization and did not pump effectively, so the AICD would treat future dysrhythmias by detecting them and delivering a jolt of electricity to depolarize his heart. The goal of the electrophysiology team during this procedure was to recreate the heart condition that caused Frank to die and monitor how the AICD responded.

I was one of the critical care nurses on the team, and my role was to assist in the procedure by monitoring

---

1. In this book, names and identifying details have been changed to protect the privacy of individuals.

Frank and defibrillating him externally if the AICD failed. I applied the large adhesive defibrillation pads to Frank's chest and back. These external pads detected the rhythm of Frank's heart, and I would use them to shock him if needed. "Beep...beep...beep...." The cardiac monitor on the external defibrillator came to life.

"Frank," I said, "I am going to start an IV in your right arm and give you a sedative to help you relax."

Nervously, Frank replied, "OK."

"Next, I am going to place this computer mouse-like device over your AICD, and the cord will be connected to this computer. This will allow us to monitor, control, and adjust your AICD. You will also see some new faces joining us. The anesthesiologist you met earlier, the representative from the company that made your defibrillator, and, of course, Dr. Jones."

As I was talking to Frank, Dr. Jones and the other personnel walked into the lab. Dr. Jones went to Frank, placed his hand on his shoulder, gave him a reassuring smile, and then looked over at me. "Chris, is Frank ready?"

"All set," I replied.

The anesthesiologist talked to Frank a moment and started to inject a milky anesthetic into the intravenous port in his right arm. Frank was unresponsive in a matter of moments. Then the anesthesiologist inserted a plastic apparatus in Frank's mouth and started to administer oxygen. He assessed Frank and told Dr. Jones that we were ready to proceed with the testing.

The electrical engineer from the defibrillator company pushed some buttons on the bedside computer linked to the AICD via the wand. "Dr. Jones," said the representative, "I am going to start pacing the heart." Dr. Jones gave a nod.

"Beep…beep…beep…." The beeps on the monitor sounded closer and closer together until finally we heard one long "beeeeeeee…."

"Clear!" said Dr. Jones.

We heard a *snap* as the AICD sent a jolt of electricity through Frank's heart, and we watched his body flop on the table. Then there was a seeming eternity of silence as we gazed with anticipation at the flat line on the monitor. Then, one by one, heart waves appeared, and the reassuring "beep…beep…beep…" started.

The word that describes my early years in the medical profession, when I had many experiences like this one, is intensity. I was a highly charged individual who lived for code blues, but all of that has since changed. It all started in 1989 when I enlisted in the army. I went to the recruiter an installer of heating and ventilation ducts and came out a medical specialist. I took the army aptitude test and qualified as a 91B, the job equivalent of a civilian emergency medical technician (EMT). I went off to basic training in South Carolina and then on for advanced medical training in Texas. The army stationed me in Germany, and I served a mechanized infantry company as its medic. After discharge, I worked as a medical technician at the Veterans Administration Medical Center (VAMC). While I worked at the VAMC, I became acquainted with some men working as nurses. Motivated by their example and military tuition reimbursement, I enrolled in a nursing program, graduated, took the exams to become board certified, and officially entered the nursing profession.

All of this was nearly a quarter of a century ago, but now, instead of a career in the intense scene of critical care, I am counseling and caring for people at the end of their lives.

My calling to the pastorate led me into the world of hospice and palliative care, and it caused me to think more deeply about modern medicine in light of Scripture.[2] Years before my calling to the pastorate, the Holy Spirit used a fellow student in nursing school to lead me to Jesus. By God's grace, I was born again through my friend's persistent witness, and a few years later, I sensed a call to the ministry. During this time, I continued working as a nurse in various capacities, but I also enrolled in a theological school. After completing these studies, I was encouraged by the elders at the church I attended to apply to seminary. Eventually, I graduated from seminary and was ordained. I served a congregation in Pennsylvania, and then the Lord burdened my heart with a desire to unite my medical and theological education and experience.

My burden stemmed from two major issues. First, my medical education and work in the health-care field exposed me to a worldview distinct from modern medical science that is radically antibiblical. I call this worldview *modern medicine*, and it is different from medical science. Modern medicine possesses guiding philosophical principles, whereas medical science is merely an empirical method. All the sciences require a philosophical

---

2. *Palliative care* is specialized medical care for people with serious illnesses. It focuses on providing patients with relief from symptoms, pain, and the stress of an illness. Unlike hospice care, it is appropriate for patients at all stages of diseases and for those suffering from curable and chronic diseases.

foundation to build on, and medical science is no different. Modern medicine has chosen to build its science on the pillars of naturalism, humanism, agnosticism, and evolution. As I pursued my theological education and continued to interact with the health-care field, I started to see how these underpinnings challenged supernaturalism, theism, absolutism, and redemption, major pillars of the Christian faith. I also encountered numerous Christians accepting these modern medical assumptions at varying levels.

For example, I encounter Christians who unwittingly embrace a view of the person that does not recognize the existence of an immaterial soul, or mind, to use a modern term. Modern medicine sees the brain as the substrate to the mind, so it assumes a view of the person called materialism, or monism. This view is over against the traditional Christian view, which is dualism (materialism/immaterialism [Gen. 2:7]). One major implication for Christians who embrace this view is an assumption that medical technology that analyzes the brain (a material entity) can provide information about the mind (an immaterial entity). In essence, Christians who believe this is possible are accepting that medical science has created a device that could be considered a "soul detector." Most Christians would think this sounds silly. Yet the determination of death (i.e., the absence of a soul) in an unresponsive individual depends partly on data gathered from an instrument called an electroencephalogram (EEG) that records the lack of electrical activity in the brain. The ethical implications for accepting this as an indicator of death are serious for Christians, as I will point out in a later chapter.

I also encounter Christians who have adopted the pervasive mindset that it is God's will for them to pursue aggressive, life-prolonging medical treatment to extreme ends. In a book unrelated to the subject of health care, focused on basic Bible doctrine, titled *Great Words*, by Rev. Jack L. Arnold, the author says, "We use all means at our disposal to prolong life." This assumption reflects the view of some in our contemporary culture, but not of the Bible. Jesus' pursuit in life was not to live as long as possible; rather, it was to do the will of His Father (Matt. 26:39). In fact, He willingly accepted His death at the relatively young age of thirty-three! The Bible instructs us repeatedly to remember our mortality and prepare for death (Luke 12:15–21; James 4:13–15), and it does not suggest we prolong our life at all costs; to do so may lead to the idolatrous worship of our life and to embracing medical practices that are unethical, a topic we will consider in chapter 1. Today, I find that many Christians live for this life because they believe God wants them to live on, using "all means at [their] disposal."

The choices Christians make are a matter of the heart, and I know from experience how difficult decisions regarding medical treatment are. There are no easy answers to life-and-death questions. My goal in this book is not to impose my convictions on others but rather to help Christians rethink how they are using modern medicine. In this book, I will show repeatedly how a biblical approach to medical science conflicts with modern medicine and how this poses serious challenges for Christians today. Both the worldview of modern medicine and Christianity offer definitions of our humanity, explain why we get sick and die, hold out healing and hope, and speak about the hereafter, but because the foundations for their belief systems are completely different, they cannot help but clash. As with all things in the world, Christians need to "walk circumspectly" (Eph. 5:15) and not be led astray through "philosophy and empty deceit, according to the tradition of men, according to the basic principles of the world, and not according to Christ" (Col. 2:8). This is no less true when Christians engage the world of modern medicine.

In light of the prevalent philosophy of modern medicine, it is time for Christians to step back and ask themselves this question: What did the apostle Paul really mean when he wrote, "For to me, to live is Christ, and to die is gain" (Phil. 1:21)? Are we to assume this was simply a Christian cliché thoughtlessly penned by the great missionary apostle? Did Paul really mean that it was better for him to die than live? The context for the passage indicates the latter. In verse 23 he wrote, "I... desire to depart and be with Christ, which is far better." Paul preferred to die, not because he desired death, but because after he died, he would be with Jesus.

This should cause us to pause, reflect, and ask ourselves if we share this same aspiration. Do we really believe it is better for us to die than live? It is easy to say "to live is Christ, and to die is gain" when we are healthy, life is going well, and death is not around the next corner, but what about when we are face-to-face with death? Will we still say, "For to me, to live is Christ, and to die is gain"?

Paul recognized that the medicine of his day—and there was an elaborate medical system even then—did not have the answers humanity longed for, nor does the medicine of our day. Jesus did—and He still does! The sad reality is that while Christians today believe this is true, their actions sometimes testify to the opposite when it comes to medical or surgical treatment. In my twenty years' experience in the health-care field, I have encountered many Christians who seek curative treatment to extreme ends. Their actions say to scoffing unbelievers, "I live for myself in the name of Jesus, and I avoid my death at all costs." For Christians whose hope is really in the ability of modern medicine to heal and prolong life, Jesus is only a miracle man or coping aide. Death has no advantage for them, and by their choices they demonstrate that they do not live for Christ in the here and now. This recurrent observation compelled me to write this book.

Compassionate Jesus: Rethinking the Christian's Approach to Modern Medicine addresses what it means for Christians to live for Christ while they make use of modern medical science and how death is still great gain for them. Amazing advancements have been made in medical science in the last century, and, as a result, modern medicine has developed its own distinctive character and philosophical approach to illness, disease, and death. In the twenty-first century, hospitals, not churches, have become the places most people in the United States look to for healing and hope. This is tragic, because the church provides the only answer for everlasting healing and hope. Jesus has a lot to say about the way we understand and use medical science, and from His teaching we are able to develop a compassionate health-care model rooted in His redemptive work that is relevant today—a model based on assumptions radically different from those of modern medicine.

A shift has occurred today, and somehow aggressive, life-saving medical treatment that developed in the 1970s has become associated with compassionate care, even in the Christian mindset. Perhaps this shift is rooted in the Good Samaritan law, which requires health-care professionals to do everything in their power to save and prolong life, but this is not what Jesus taught in the parable of the Good Samaritan. In the story, Jesus spoke about a man showing compassion for someone in a medical crisis by tending wounds, managing suffering, providing for needs, and facilitating a safe environment. The emphasis is not on aggressive procedures to prolong life at all costs but rather compassionate intervention to treat suffering and symptoms. Throughout the Gospels, Jesus communicated that He was the true cure for illness, disease, and death, and He taught us to show compassion. The aggressive agenda of modern medicine challenges Jesus' answer to illness, disease, and death in many ways. So it is the Christian's responsibility to answer this challenge by advancing Jesus' "health-care agenda" in the United States and abroad.

The Christian recognizes that nothing happens by chance. Behind every illness, disease, tragedy, and death rests the triune God's eternal plan of redemption, which is the foundation for true health, wellness, and life. No life experience is a random, fortuitous event that catches God by surprise. How all of this unfolds in time is a great mystery to us, but the Bible is emphatically clear: God has planned every illness, disease, and tragedy we will experience in life—and even the very moment we will die (Eccl. 3:1–11; Eph. 1:3–14). Therefore, our goal in life is to study this plan in light of Scripture and connect our lives to it repeatedly in order to experience true healing and hope. Put simply, our mission in life is to align our will with the will of God and use medical and surgical treatments as the instruments He intended them to be. Jesus prescribed prayer to help us do this; prayer is God's medicine. It is through the activity of prayer we enter into the presence of the Father and Son, motivated by the Holy Spirit, to express our heartfelt desires, bear one another's burdens, and seek wisdom to understand the triune God's purpose for our lives as we come face-to-face with affliction, calamity, and our mortality.

Spirit-dependent prayer will make us bold in the face of death. Indeed, we will be able to confess with Paul that death is "great gain," and we will use modern medical science the way God intended—we will "live for Christ." This is the ultimate goal for this book. Jesus teaches us that death is a positive transition for the Christian, but for those who trust in modern medicine, it is the beginning of eternal hopelessness, sickness, suffering, and death. Hell awaits those who do not live for Christ. Jesus has entrusted the Christian with an unpopular mission to warn people about hell, expose the false teachings modern medicine offers in its place, and proclaim boldly His exclusive resurrection answer to death and hell.

Throughout this book, I will encourage readers to rethink their approach to modern medicine. In chapter 1, I will develop a Christian worldview for modern medical science, giving the name of this approach *compassionate health care.* In the second chapter, I will consider the advances of medical science and the blessing they have been for many, but I will also consider some of the challenges these advancements pose to Christians. In chapter 3, I will consider how to use modern medical science biblically and develop principles to engage modern medicine today. The fourth chapter focuses on prayer, first by considering the example of Job, and then moving on to provide suggestions on how to pray in the midst of illness, disease, and death. In the last chapter, I will consider the modern hospice movement in the United States and some of the major challenges this movement poses to Christians at end of life.

It is time to step back and rethink our approach to modern medicine in light of biblical teaching and sincerely ask ourselves two important questions: (1) Are we living for Christ in the midst of a medical crisis? (2) Do we really see our death as great gain as we look in hope to Christ? It is my prayer that *Compassionate Jesus* will help us answer these questions and equip us to live for Christ, even in the face of illness, disease, tragedy, and death.

Chapter 1

God's Plan and Compassionate Health Care

Several years ago, my sister died in a tragic automobile accident. The shocking news devastated my family, especially my mother. In her deep and very real pain, she repeatedly asked, "Why would God do this?" I sat silently in her bedroom with her, my arm around her. Later that night, I fell on my knees in prayer, asking God why this had happened, just as my mother had. In the still sadness, the groans of my heart did the praying, and Genesis 18:25 came repeatedly to mind: "Shall not the Judge of all the earth do right?" I wondered why the Holy Spirit had brought this passage to mind, but after prayerful reflection, peace and comfort filled my pain-stricken soul.

Genesis 18–19 is the famous passage in which Abraham barters with God regarding His promised judgment on the wicked cities Sodom and Gomorrah. Abraham asks God to spare the good people in the city, especially his nephew Lot and his family. In essence, Abraham is saying that if God is just, He cannot destroy the good with the bad. Abraham begins bartering with God and asks Him if He will spare the city for the sake of fifty good people. God agrees, but Abraham remembers just how wicked these cities are, and, after lowering the count several times, ends up asking God to spare the city for the sake of ten people. Finally, Abraham realizes that no one in the city is good, not even Lot. God destroys Sodom and Gomorrah, but He mercifully delivers Lot and his family.

As I meditated on this passage, I realized that I didn't have to wonder why my sister died because I already knew the answer. Abraham's conclusion, although difficult to accept, was true: none of us deserves better than death, for we are all bad people before an impeccably good Judge. Both the Old and New Testaments teach that sin corrupts everyone, making us all guilty before God, the Judge of all the earth. In Psalm 14, David writes,

> The LORD looks down from heaven upon
>   the children of men,
> To see if there are any who understand, who seek God.
> They have all turned aside,
> They have together become corrupt;
> There is none who does good,
> No, not one (vv. 2–3).

In the New Testament, Paul quotes this passage in Romans 3, linking both Testaments' views of sin, corruption, and guilt:

> As it is written:
> "There is none righteous, no, not one;
> There is none who understands;
> There is none who seeks after God.
> They have all turned aside;
> They have together become unprofitable;
> There is none who does good, no, not one" (vv. 10–12).

The reality is that we deserve every illness, disease, sickness, tragedy, disease, and death that comes our way—and never anything better. We live on borrowed time, and day after day the merciful Judge spares us, as He spared Lot and his family, until finally one day, in His timing, our deserved sentence of death arrives (Heb. 9:27). "The wages of sin is death," writes Paul (Rom. 6:23). Every day, whether we choose to recognize it or not, we live in the presence of a sovereign God who is in complete control of our lives (Ps. 115:3), who is the epitome of justice (Ps. 89:14), and who delights to show mercy (Ps. 111:4).

Rabbi Harold Kushner wrote *When Bad Things Happen to Good People* as an attempt to make sense of his son's death from a rare disease. Kushner asks the question both my mother and I asked: Why would God do this? This book is his extended answer. Kushner concluded that if God could prevent human suffering and death He would, but the reality is that He cannot. In Kushner's world, humans deserve better, and God wants to give us better, but He can't because the fates tie His hands. But the sovereign God revealed in Scripture, who is not the deity of Rabbi Kushner, is not subject to the fates. He shows us mercy daily, until finally, one day, He takes back our borrowed breath (Ps. 104:29).

As I mourned my sister's death, peace and comfort filled my soul because I knew God was in complete control. Her death rested entirely in God's hands. Could there be any better hands for a loved one to be in? Ultimately, the merciful and just Creator decided, according to His perfect timetable, to take my sister. She had returned to Him (Eccl. 12:7), the one who is merciful and just, and we needed to remember, reflect, reform our thoughts, and stand in awe of this majestic, awesome, magnificent God.

I learned three important things about God that evening. First, God is merciful. Although we deserve death, He lets us live. God gave my sister a half-century, and her life and eternal well-being rested in His mercy. Second, God is just. He will always do what is equitable. He is not capricious and is always true to Himself, and what my sister did or did not do will not ultimately change His verdict regarding her. Third, God is in absolute control, and everything that happens in our lives has purpose and meaning. Ultimately, using contingent events, God orchestrated my sister's fatal accident entirely for His own incomprehensible purposes.

When we embrace this biblical perspective on sickness, tragedy, and death, we recognize that what happens is not about us—it's about God and His redemptive plan for our lives, which we will explain in more detail later in this chapter. We will understand that when sickness and death confront us, these are the better questions: What is God teaching me? How does this situation fit into God's plan? How can I draw closer to God in the midst of this? How can I align myself with God's plan? We will start to understand more clearly that we are part of a mysterious narrative that is much more complex than our infinitesimal minds can fathom—a redemptive plan that God graciously allows us to participate in and peek into here and there. It is this perspective that must provide the context for Christians when they consider modern medical science and what it has to offer.

Prolonging Life: Counting the Costs

In March 2009, a study in the *Journal of the American Medical Association* reported that those who regularly prayed were more than three times more likely to receive intensive life-prolonging care than those who relied least on religion. The article also said that religious people were less likely to have advance medical directives such as living wills and do-not-resuscitate (DNR) order and were more likely to pursue aggressive treatment to prolong life at all costs. These findings do not appear surprising until you look at the patient group for the study. The study followed 345 terminally ill cancer patients. These people, in the opinion of the medical community, had six months or less to live, and curative treatment was futile. The article did not break down the religious groups but focused only on those who regularly prayed.

In the same month, a *Los Angeles Times* article focused specifically on a sixty-six-year-old Christian woman who was diagnosed with stage 4 breast cancer. The title of the article was "Aligning a Medical Treatment Plan with God's Plan: Faith Drives Some Patients to Fight, and Suffer More at the End." The woman had had a mastectomy and hormone treatments to suppress the tumors, but, she said, "The Lord was just telling me, 'They're not being aggressive enough.'" She traveled three hundred miles to an expensive cancer specialty clinic in Michigan, where she had a bone marrow transplant and ended up on life support. She survived the awful ordeal and said, "Had the Lord not sent me there, I don't think I would be alive today."

Is it really faithfulness, or is something else compelling Christians to pursue aggressive medical treatment to prolong life at all costs? After all, the sixth commandment says, "You shall not murder" (Ex. 20:13), and by way of application we understand this commandment to mean we have an obligation to preserve life. Does this mean God expects me, like the woman in the *Times* article, to exhaust every possible medical treatment to prolong my life? The answer is yes and no. Yes, God wants us to prolong our lives, provided it is according to His will. No, God does not want us to prolong our lives if it is not according to His will. Whether we live or die is not the issue (Rom. 14:8); the issue is whether we are doing the will of God. If our motives are self-serving and the treatment we receive to prolong our lives will take another person's life, or even our own, then it is not God's will for us to have the treatment. Life is a sacred gift the Creator of all life gives, so it needs careful handling, but we must not worship it.

I have encountered many Christians who focus more on life and the victory over death offered by advances in medical science than on Christ's victory over death and the spiritual life He gives. They share the mindset of Dr. John Dunlop, a Christian medical doctor, who wrote in his book *Finishing Well to the Glory of God*, "If we are viewing death as an enemy to be defeated, we will want all possible treatments. But if death is near and treatment options are less attractive, we will view death as a defeated enemy." These sentences seem to frame the Christian's view of life and death in light of medical advances and individual choice based on available treatment options. In a chapter titled "Make an Appropriate Use of Technology," Dunlop seeks to develop principles for the proper use of medical technology for Christians, but he urges his readers to consider treatment in the context of a benefit-versus-futility construct. This normally ends up with the approach that translates into "exhaust all possible treatment options to prolong life, and then throw in the towel when death is no longer avoidable." The reality, however, is a sick and dying Christian can reject medical science completely and still look death in the eye and say, "Defeated foe, Christ rose from the dead; I'm alive, even though I am dying!" Victory over death and true life is in Jesus—not in modern medical science and prolongation of life—and physical healing for the Christian awaits His return.

Times may change, but Jesus and His accomplishments are always the same. Whether it was the patriarchs of old looking forward in faith through types and shadows for the coming of Jesus, or the apostles gazing in faith into the eyes of Jesus, or we today seeing Jesus by faith in the pages of Scripture, "Jesus Christ is the same yesterday, today, and forever" (Heb. 13:8). The issues surrounding life and death are not new either. When Jesus was living in this world, He allowed His friend Lazarus to die rather than come immediately to heal him, which confused Mary, Martha, the disciples, and onlookers (see John 11). The consensus of the people was, "Could not this Man, who opened the eyes of the blind, also have kept this man from dying?" (John 11:37). Jesus had something greater planned, however: "This sickness is not unto death," said Jesus, "but for the glory of God, that the Son of God may be glorified through it" (John 11:4). The glory of God took precedence over Jesus' healing Lazarus to prolong his life, even though it was in His power to do so. In fact, it was in Jesus' power to heal and prolong the lives of every sick person He met, but He did not. We know that because Jesus was perfectly righteous, He did not sin, so He kept the sixth commandment perfectly, even though He did not heal all sick people.

Jesus, the apostles, and the Old Testament prophets performed healing and resurrection miracles, but the truth is that all of those who were healed and resurrected died one day. God had something else in mind when He allowed these miracles to occur. Their primary purpose was to testify to the power, identity, and message of God. They were signposts that pointed to Christ, His promised hope of healing, and His ultimate victory over death at the end of this age (John 20:30–31).

Scripture teaches us that something even greater than health and physical life is at stake in this world: the glory of God in redemption as revealed in Jesus Christ. Still today, God's glory takes precedence over physical healing in our lives, and the Christian who truly understands this principle will see that the goals of modern medicine oppose God's ultimate redemptive purpose in Jesus Christ. Let's take a closer look at a critical passage in Ephesians to get a better understanding of God's plan to bring Himself glory through the drama of redemption.

Jesus Christ—the Same Yesterday, Today, and Forever

Ephesians 1:3–14 succinctly reveals God's glory in the drama of redemption. Understanding this passage is crucial, because it sets the context for our lives today, just as it did in every time and place in human history. The entire theme of Ephesians is "one people in Christ before time began." The first chapter, like a rolled-up carpet, is God's plan before time began.

Paul begins with praise: "Blessed be the God and Father of our Lord Jesus Christ, who has blessed us with every spiritual blessing in the heavenly places in Christ, just as He chose us in Him before the foundation of the world, that we should be holy and without blame before Him in love" (vv. 3–4). The first thing to notice is God the Father determined before He created anything to choose particular people in Christ. Further, Paul goes on to say in verse 5 that before time began God the Father planned to have an adoptive family. Note second that God the Father is the operative force in all of this as the plan unrolls in time (vv. 4–10). Third, the plan of God the Father includes "all things" in heaven and on earth—not some things, but everything, even the seemingly insignificant and mundane details of life (v. 10). The fourth thing to notice is the plan of God the Father is still unrolling, like a carpet, today (v. 10).

Next, Paul's praise indicates that God the Father did all of this in collaboration with His Son. God the Father, in collaboration with God the Son, thought up this mysterious plan before it ever happened. Theologians call this agreement the covenant of redemption, or council of peace. It was a pact made between the Father, Son, and Holy Spirit before time began (cf. Zech. 6:12–13). In Ephesians 1:3–14 Paul is describing the role of Christ in the covenant. At least fourteen times Paul directly or indirectly indicates the plan was accomplished "in Him," that is in Christ. God the Father does not do anything without the mediation of God the Son—this is a part of the agreement made before time began.

Finally, Paul's praise refers to "us," but not to everyone. To whom is Paul referring? In the immediate context, it is obvious that Paul is referring to himself and to those who "heard the word of truth" at Ephesus (v. 13). The "us" also includes others, according to Paul—not only Paul and some who are at Ephesus but also the Jews and Gentiles of every generation who are redeemed in Jesus Christ (Eph. 3:6). The words of Peter come to mind in the Pentecost sermon: "For the promise is to you and to your children, and to all who are afar off, as many as the Lord our God will call" (Acts 2:39).

Ephesians 1:3–14 says that the ultimate purpose of God is to heal people in Jesus Christ and restore them to human wholeness by making them part of one new body, the body of Christ, the church. Before God created anything, He instituted the plan of redemption to glorify Himself. This is not only the theme of the entire Bible, but it also undergirds the entire story of the world: history, politics, economics, philosophy, law, religion, science, literature, and aesthetics. It is also the thread that runs through every person's life, whether he is Christian or not. Every breath, heartbeat, thought, action, and—yes— every catastrophe, tragedy, illness, disease, and death that occurs ties into this plan in some mysterious way. It forms the backbone for the triune God's creation. Everything hangs from this one overarching purpose in one way or another, and everything that comes to pass flows out of it in one way or another. It is a plan calculated to do one thing: *bring God glory.* This is the ultimate message in

Scripture that is the same yesterday, today, and forever, and it is the common thread uniting us with brothers and sisters of bygone ages. We share the same redemptive purpose, the same Christ, and the same struggles.

The Cult of Asclepius and the Worship of Health

In Revelation, we see that Christians in the apostolic age already had lost sight of God's overarching redemptive purpose and struggled with the same idolatrous pursuits that we face today. During the days of the apostle John, a popular temple in Pergamum, which today is Bergama, Turkey, was devoted to Asclepius, the Greek god of healing. Pergamum was the capital of the ancient Attalid kingdom for more than a century (263–133 BC). In 133 BC, Attalus III bequeathed it to the Romans, and it became the first Roman seat in Asia Minor. The inhabitants of Pergamum worshiped four primary deities: Zeus, Athena, Dionysus, and Asclepius, all of whose images appear on excavated coinage from that area. Asclepius, however, with his promise of healing, was exalted above them all, the record of antiquity suggests. And today, Asclepius's symbol of healing, a staff entwined with a serpent, has been adopted by the medical community as its icon (the medical caduceus).

In the first century, the temple of Asclepius in Pergamum was renowned for its healing. Even the emperor Domitian paid tribute to the temple. In *Silvae*, Statius (c. AD 45–96), the ancient Roman poet, wrote, "The [emperor is sending his] tresses...to Asclepius at Pergamum, together with a mirror and a jeweled box." Statius praised Asclepius: "The shrine at Pergamum, where the great helper of the sick is present to aid, and stays the hurrying fates and bends, [is] a kindly deity, o'er his health-bringing snake." Philostratus (c. AD 170–247), an Athenian sophist, wrote an interesting account called the *Life of Apollonius of Tyana*. He mentions the popularity of Asclepius in Pergamum and Crete in this story when he says "all of Asia flocks" to his temples.

Writing to the church at Pergamum in Revelation 2:13, John records the words of Jesus: "I know...where you dwell, where Satan's throne is. And you hold fast to My name." Christians were holding fast against Satan's rule "where Satan's throne is," the place in Pergamum where they were living. The Bible tells us that Satan dwells and exercises his rule in the spiritual realm (Eph. 2:2). In essence, Jesus is saying, "I know where you Christians live, at the place where Satan (Asclepius) has his throne (cf. Rev. 12:9). In the past, you held fast to My name and did not deny your faith, even under Roman persecution. You did this in the place where Satan is presently dwelling. Now, some of you are showing allegiance to Satan! The healing power of Asclepius has captured you." We can conclude from these verses that the satanic dwelling place of Revelation 2:13 is the temple of Asclepius, where the people of that day would turn for healing. Even the Christians were falling prey to Asclepius's challenge to Jesus' promise of healing.

Another important indicator that John was pointing to Asclepius is the mention of a white stone in Revelation 2:17. In antiquity, people used stones for various purposes, such as casting a vote. But there is also evidence to suggest that white stones, in particular, were used for initiation into the temple of Asclepius. The priest wrote a patient's name on the white stone, and then the patient would present it as an offering to Asclepius. Jesus says that He will give another white stone with a new name written on it, one offered to God. Throughout the book of Revelation a new name is synonymous with new life (cf. Rev. 3:5) and, therefore, the promise of true health, wellness, and life to come in Christ (Rev. 21:4). Those who overcome the idolatrous hopes of this present age will receive these promises, as Revelation 2:17 indicates.

Beginning around 500 BC, the cult of Asclepius grew and gathered a great following. Sick people from all over the Mediterranean world flocked to the god's temples, driven by his promise of healing. Today, although weathered by time, the temple of Asclepius stands in Pergamum as an enduring testimony to the powerful influence Asclepius and his priests and healers and their entire medical enterprise had on the Mediterranean world during the days of the apostle John. Pergamum was the place to go for health, healing, and hope in the ancient world, just as many go to hospitals today. Curative medical techniques and institutions may change, but the spirit of idolatrous hope is always the same.

The major issue John was addressing with the church at Pergamum was idolizing health, wellness, and life. He was addressing the issue of Christians professing hope in Christ for healing but really trusting the institutions around them for it. More specifically, he was addressing Christians who were seeking hope at the temple of Asclepius and not the church. John is not saying, as the biblical witness clearly illustrates, that it is wrong to seek

medical treatment. What John is saying is that when
hope in healing is the focus of a person's life, then Jesus
will be less important, and when this happens, idolatry
prevails. Idolatry is timeless, and it comes about when
God and His ways are secondary to man's fears, desires,
and hopes.

A biblical example of a person who idolized the medical community is King Asa (910–869 BC). Asa's story
is one of triumph and tragedy. He reigned in Judah for
forty-one years, and for most of those years he "did what
was right in the eyes of the LORD" (1 Kings 15:11). Asa
brought civil and religious reforms to the nation. He rid
Judah of its pagan influences, rebuilt its cities, and established its military prowess. The defining passage for Asa
is 2 Chronicles 15:2: "The LORD is with you while you are
with Him.... If you forsake Him, He will forsake you."
All was peace in Asa's reign until the thirty-sixth year,
when Baasha, king of Israel, attacked him. This was the
beginning of Asa's downfall, because in fear he turned
away from God and trusted in the power of men. Three
years following the battle, he was afflicted with a foot
ailment, perhaps a vascular disease that led to sepsis or a
fatal blood clot, that killed him (1 Kings 15:23). "Yet in his
disease he did not seek the LORD," writes the chronicler,
"but the physicians" (2 Chron. 16:12). Asa died two years
later as an embittered man trapped in idolatry, seeking
hope and healing from the medical institution of his day.

Idolatry has many faces, but the root is always the
same: God and His ways are secondary to man and his
ways. Why are Christians today, like King Asa and those
living in Pergamum, tempted to idolize medicine? First,

many are afraid to die. It is easy for us to express bold-ness concerning death when it is only a distant concept, but fear can set in when it becomes a stark reality. Sec-ond, many are addicted to this world. They love their life, family, church, job, and comforts so much that they do not want to leave them, even if it means going to be with Jesus in heaven. Third, many have unwittingly absorbed worldly attitudes about modern medicine without ques-tioning its value, truth, ethics, or goals. Fourth, there are many who see modern medicine as a neutral sci-ence. They give little or no thought to the philosophical underpinnings of modern medicine and how they influ-ence the care they receive. Fifth, there are many who have a low or confused view of God's providence. Rather than attempting to understand God's "good" purpose in sickness (Rom. 8:28), they seek treatment first and then attempt to fit God's purpose into theirs. We must be on guard against human ways of thinking that attempt to supplant God and His ways so that we don't fall prey to the sin of idolatry.

Christians have to be wary of bowing the knee to Asclepius. Although Asclepius was a mythological figure and any Christian, even from the first century, would think it absurd to bow to him, the Greek god's spirit lives on in modern medicine, and his satanic power hypno-tizes many Christians today. The magnetic force of hope in health, happiness, and life in the here and now and the attempt to avoid illness, disease, suffering, and death at all costs draws people. It is a subtle but deviant spirit that can easily deceive followers of Christ (see 2 Cor. 11:14). Jesus said, "I have come that they may have life, and that they may have it more abundantly" (John 10:10), yet sometimes Christians forget Jesus also said that fullness and healing will never be found in this life, but only in a restored life to come (Matt. 6:20–21). Jesus came into the world to bring spiritual healing at present and physical healing at a future date, so the way the Christian understands and applies medical science will be different from the rest of the world, which clings to the fabled promises of Asclepius and modern medicine.

The Year of the Lord's Favor

While the world seeks Asclepius's favor, Christians look to Jesus and "the year of the Lord's favor," a major epoch in the triune God's eternal plan of redemption. The Bible is full of contrasts, and one major distinction is that all things are completed in Jesus, but they are not yet finished by Him. It is the difference between D-day, which secured the Allied forces' victory over Nazi Germany in the Second World War, and the actual completion of the war in Europe on V-E Day. Encapsulated in the year of the Lord's favor is what Jesus achieved during His incarnation and the implications this has for Christians today as they wait with eager anticipation for the full realization of His victory when He returns.

Take a journey back in time with me as I set the context for Jesus' incarnation and the year of the Lord's favor that He ushered in as the prophet Isaiah promised (Isa. 61:2). The emperor Augustus (27 BC–AD 14) is on the imperial throne in Rome (Luke 2:1), and the temple of Asclepius in Pergamum has been providing medical care for hundreds of years. The late Hippocrates of Cos

(460–370 BC) has sent his medical craft throughout the known world for others to learn. Luke, the evangelist, physician, and writer of the second gospel and Acts, is undoubtedly educated in the ways of Hippocrates and Asclepius, yet he does not direct his readers to find healing in them but rather in Christ. In Palestine—a small, obscure, but troublesome region in Rome's empire—a child was born, writes Luke (2:7). The year of the Lord's favor had arrived; Jesus Christ, the healing hope for humanity, had entered the world as Isaiah prophesied.

Luke's gospel reveals the mission Jesus came to accomplish. After Jesus' anointing by the Holy Spirit (3:21–22) and His battle with Satan in the Judean wilderness (4:1–13), He returned to His hometown, Nazareth, and worshiped at a local synagogue. In Luke 4:16–19, we read:

> As His custom was, He went into the synagogue on the Sabbath day, and stood up to read. And He was handed the book of the prophet Isaiah. And when He had opened the book, He found the place where it was written: "The Spirit of the LORD is upon Me, because He has anointed Me to preach the gospel to the poor; He has sent Me to heal the brokenhearted, to proclaim liberty to the captives and recovery of sight to the blind, to set at liberty those who are oppressed; to proclaim the acceptable year of the LORD."

Jesus' mission was threefold: (1) He came to preach; (2) He came to set people free from bondage to sin; and (3) He came to heal. He came "to proclaim the acceptable year of the LORD," or, in some Bible translations, "the year of the Lord's favor." By His incarnation, Jesus began a process of renewal through His preaching of repentance, freeing people from sinful bondage, and healing their human brokenness.

There was a fourth aspect to Jesus' mission not mentioned at the synagogue in Nazareth. As Jesus read from the scroll of Isaiah, He stopped midsentence. Isaiah 61:2 goes on to say that He will also proclaim "the day of vengeance of our God." The "day of vengeance" is an Old Testament expression referring to Jesus' second coming, a time of final judgment yet to arrive and the last great epoch in redemptive history. It is a time distinct from Jesus' incarnation, His first coming, the year of the Lord's favor. On the day of His second coming, Jesus will deal the final blow to Satan, sin, sickness, and death. Everyone who ever existed will stand before Him for judgment on this day (Rev. 20:11–15). Those who trusted and hoped in His healing provision will go to heaven, but those who sought the favor of Asclepius will be condemned to hell. After the final judgment, Jesus will bring to completion the process of healing and restoration He started on earth during His incarnation.

By His incarnation, Jesus provided a way for full restoration from illness, disease, and death today, but He has yet to complete the process. We live in a time characterized as already / not yet. Jesus has completed all things necessary for human healing, wholeness, and restoration, but He has not yet finished the process because the day of vengeance of our God has yet to arrive. It is important to understand this distinction, because it is in this context we are to view illness, disease, and death today. True healing—that is, healing at its fullest extent—will arrive after Jesus returns, unleashing on earth the full blessings He achieved by His life, death, and resurrection. Physical healing is not the primary goal for human beings at this time; spiritual restoration leading to true health and the hope of human wholeness are.

Spiritual Healing and Hope

In Mark 2:1–12, we find one of the clearest examples of what it means to give priority to spiritual restoration over physical healing in the present. In this passage, Jesus was teaching at Peter's home in Capernaum, and a capacity crowd filled the house. Four men carrying a paralytic on a cheap mattress attempted to push their way into Peter's house to see Jesus, but they were unsuccessful. The eager men changed plans and ascended a stairway on the outside of the house, carrying the paralytic to the roof. After they climbed onto the roof, they found the area above Jesus and dug a hole in the straw and clay. After they broke through the roof and widened the hole, they hastily lowered the paralytic to Jesus.

As the pieces of straw-laced clay fell, dry, chalky smoke filled the room, and the shocked people looked up. With dust-filled eyes, they gazed upon the crippled man on the mattress, lowered from the ceiling to Jesus. Mark writes:

> When Jesus saw their faith, He said to the paralytic, "Son, your sins are forgiven you." And some of the scribes were sitting there and reasoning in their hearts, "Why does this Man speak blasphemies like this? Who can forgive sins but God alone?" But immediately, when Jesus perceived in His spirit

that they reasoned thus within themselves, He said to them, "Why do you reason about these things in your hearts? Which is easier, to say to the paralytic, 'Your sins are forgiven you,' or to say, 'Arise, take up your bed and walk'? But that you may know that the Son of Man has power on earth to forgive sins"—He said to the paralytic, "I say to you, arise, take up your bed, and go to your house." Immediately he arose, took up the bed, and went out in the presence of them all, so that all were amazed and glorified God, saying, "We never saw anything like this!" (vv. 5–12).

The first thing to notice in this passage is that Jesus responded to the faith of the men. They believed Jesus had the power, authority, and ability to restore the paralytic, so they were determined to see Him. Second, Jesus did not initially heal the paralytic; first, He forgave his sins. In so doing, He taught that a priority exists. The man's spiritual condition took precedence over his physical condition. It is at this point we see the clear line of demarcation between the mission of Jesus at His incarnation, the year of the Lord's favor, and second coming, the day of vengeance of our God. Jesus has come to set people free from sin at present, not to heal them physically, and to point them to human wholeness that is yet to come. Third, Jesus healed the man physically, not merely to heal him but to testify to His authority to forgive sins. Jesus was proving to the Jewish religious officials that He had the power to restore people spiritually and physically because He has come to proclaim the year of the Lord's favor, just as Isaiah foretold.

Living an impeccably moral life, performing miracles, doing good deeds, showing compassion, and teaching people about the glorious future hope to come were not enough for Jesus to accomplish His assigned mission, however. He needed to set us free from sin by accomplishing our salvation, so He had to accept the wages of sin, which is the sentence of death (Rom. 6:23). Part of Jesus' mission was to suffer, die, and rise from the dead (Acts 2:22–24). Jesus had to experience the death and sin we inherited from the first Adam and give us what we do not deserve—freedom and hope of healing. Jesus suffered the miseries we merited, experienced the torments we warranted, and died the death we earned on the cross. "[God] made Him who knew no sin to be sin for us," Paul wrote, "that we might become the righteousness of God in Him" (2 Cor. 5:21). Part of the remedy was Jesus' impeccable life and willing death in exchange for the believer's sin.

The other part of the remedy was Jesus' resurrection. His death was not enough because He had to rise from the grave in newness of life in order to give people healing and life. Jesus appeased God's wrath against sin on the cross, and His resurrection from the tomb certified His victory. Jesus, the second Adam, completely reversed what the first Adam did in rebelling against God, which brought sin, misery, illness, suffering, and death into the world. Paul wrote in Romans 5:12: "As through one man sin entered the world, and death through sin, and thus death spread to all men, because all sinned." Paul explains this again in 1 Corinthians 15:45: "'The first man

Adam became a living being.' The last Adam became a life-giving spirit."

After Jesus rose from the dead, providing redemption for His chosen people, He ascended into heaven and sat down at the Father's right hand, where He waits to return in glory and power. God gave Jesus full authority as the second Adam (Matt. 28:18), the representative of renewed humanity, as a reward for His faithful obedience. Eventually the day of vengeance of our God will arrive, and Jesus will return to complete the process of physical healing and spiritual restoration. He will place the capstone on redemption! Jesus will complete the mission started on the earth during the year of the Lord's favor, but until that happy and glorious day, Christ has commissioned, equipped, and empowered His disciples to continue His earthly mission to a world seeking the hopeless favor of Asclepius.

Crucial Principles and Their Implications

It is helpful to summarize seven crucial principles derived from Jesus' life, teaching, and ministry in light of the triune God's redemptive purposes that should undergird our approach to illness, disease, and death today.

1. Jesus identified with the human race by becoming human—He knows human suffering.

2. Jesus' mission in life was to proclaim the year of the Lord's favor; there is healing hope now, but it is primarily spiritual in nature.

3. Jesus provided a way for physical healing that would manifest itself fully at His second coming.

4. Jesus taught and clearly demonstrated by His actions that physical healing is secondary to spiritual restoration at present.

5. Jesus healed people physically to testify to His authority and compassion and to show forth His power and ability to restore people completely at a future date.

6. Jesus suffered, endured hellish torments, and died an awful death on our behalf to free us, at our death or at His second coming, from illness and disease.

7. Jesus rose from the dead victorious over suffering, sickness, and death as a testimony to the promise of physical healing and wholeness that is yet to come.

Hope for Healing Is in Jesus Alone

What are some of the practical implications derived from these seven principles for Christians today? The first implication gleaned from Jesus' teaching is that hope for physical healing must be exclusively in Him, and not in modern medical science, even when it offers proper and ethical means that He is pleased to bless. His healing promise will arrive at a future date. It is important to note, however, that while Jesus presented Himself as the ultimate hope for physical healing, He did not condemn health care or the people who sought it. Jesus was not averse to the medical care of His day and, therefore, by implication, to the medical care of our own. The parable of the Good Samaritan provides enduring principles we can apply to the medical care fellow human beings should show one another, which, in the parable, includes ointment, wine, bandages, and nursing care. Jesus did not criticize the woman who "had spent all her livelihood on physicians" to find healing (Luke 8:43). Rather, He allowed miraculous power to exude from His body, curing her misery and providing her with true hope. It is when Jesus' solution for healing is secondary that we deviate from His teaching and idolatry traps us.

Jesus was not averse to using naturalistic means either. In one of His healing miracles, He used dirt, spit, and water (John 9:6–7). Jesus drank wine, ate food, and permitted the pouring of aromatic oil on His head, testifying to His use of the creation to feel good (Ps. 104:15), sustain life (Matt. 6:11), and receive a special anointing (Matt. 26:7). "For every [created thing] of God is good," wrote Paul, "and nothing is to be refused if it is received with thanksgiving" (1 Tim. 4:4). God created everything, and there is nothing made by humankind that is not composed of something God created. Nothing new exists under the sun, wrote the Preacher (Eccl. 1:9). Part of God's mandate to subdue His creation includes a careful study (i.e., scientific inquiry) into the intricacies of human life, the world, and the universe and the application of these findings to aid us here and now. Thus, according to Jesus, the use of medicine, surgery, and technology to treat illness, disease, and death is perfectly legitimate, provided the means are moral, ethical, and free from idolatrous pursuit.

No Complete Physical Healing in This Life
The second implication is that physical healing will never come to complete fruition in this life. Medical science

may cure one ailment, but another will come, and eventually death will terminate human life. Medical science really treats symptoms. Modern medicine's pursuit of healing will always become futile, so there will be a point in every Christian's life when relying on modern medical science to prolong life can become an idol. The triune God will draw the line and say, "Is My hope and healing reserved for you in heaven? Or are you relying on modern medical hope and healing so that you may prolong your life on earth?" The latter may lead to a prolongation of days, but it may also mean significant temporal and, perhaps, even eternal costs for those who idolize modern medicine. Where God draws the line is not always easy to discern, but Christians need to understand the implications and goals of the medical treatment they receive so that they can make wise choices that reflect their faith in God and honor Him (some of these issues will be addressed in chapter 3).

Spiritual Restoration Takes Precedence over Physical Healing

The third implication is that spiritual restoration takes precedence over physical healing presently. Certainly, it is not wrong to pray for healing miracles, nor is it wrong to seek medical treatment. If it is God's will to heal a person miraculously, He will do so. If it is His will to heal a person through medical intervention, He will do this as well. However, it is wrong to seek healing miracles and medical treatments *merely* for the sake of physical healing. Simply stated, we must remember that it is not always God's will to grant physical healing during the year of the Lord's favor, and we need to be willing to submit ourselves to that will to avoid the sin of idolatry and all the misery it brings to others and ourselves. Jesus taught us that sin is the main problem we have to contend with today, not illness, disease, and death, which are the results, or symptoms, of sin. It is wonderful to see a sick person healed physically, whether by miracle or medical treatment, but it is equally praiseworthy to see a person persevere under affliction and die in the Lord with no curative treatment. In both instances, the Christian has experienced spiritual healing, and the testimony of God's written record has transformed his life. The Christian life is essentially a spiritual life at present characterized by faith, hope, and love.

Illness, disease, trauma, decay, aging, death, and all the evils of this present world will take their inevitable toll on all people, but the Christian can take heart because inwardly the Holy Spirit is renewing him day by day in faith, hope, and love. With the powerful influence of the Holy Spirit and the Word of God on the soul, the body can function as God originally created it, namely, to manifest humankind's original image even in the midst of sickness, suffering, and dying. This was the image Christ, the second Adam, displayed in His life, suffering, and death. The re-creative work of the Word of God and the Holy Spirit in the Christian's soul moves him toward one desire—renewal into the image of God, which is true human wholeness. This is the all-encompassing passion and ever-growing affection of every believer. If the pursuit of physical healing to prolong life interferes with this spiritually restorative process, then the pursuit of physical healing must be questioned.

Consider Ruth, a thirty-one-year-old Christian diagnosed with aggressive breast cancer. About four weeks before her diagnosis, Ruth saw her primary care physician for increasing pain, fatigue, and periodic shortness of breath. After the exam, her doctor sent her for a mammogram, which revealed several tumors in her breasts. A later full-body scan revealed metastasis throughout her body. Ruth received diagnostic and prognostic confirmation from two oncologists, and they both confirmed the grim news. The oncologist offered her treatment to prolong her life, but she refused it, so he reluctantly referred her to a home hospice agency.

Almost immediately, due to excruciating pain and the shocking news, Ruth went into a state of depression. She had dull, achy pain all over her body, but particularly in her back. Ruth's mood was flat, and she complained of feeling numb. She stayed in bed most of the time, alienated herself, and ate almost nothing. The hospice doctor started Ruth on several different medications to treat her symptoms. After two days Ruth's mood was elevated, her appetite was better, her energy level was increased, and she was nearly pain free. The side effects from the medications were minimal as well.

Ruth was able to read her Bible, pray, sing, and welcome visitors. Her pastor was involved from the beginning, and he visited once a week to counsel her and to work with the hospice team. He counseled her in the areas of faith, hope, and love and focused on the promise of physical healing to come in Christ; he also reported any changes he observed to the hospice professionals. The deacons from her church set up a visitation schedule for the members of the congregation, and they provided for some of her physical and material needs. The atmosphere in Ruth's home was joyous, warm, vibrant, and caring.

Ruth was able to sit through an entire worship service. She heard the preaching of the word, participated in a Lord's Supper, witnessed a baptism, sang praise to God, and enjoyed fellowship with her brothers and sisters in Christ. She worshiped for nearly two months before she could no longer attend services. A day after her last worship service, Ruth started to decline. Her body was weakening, and the medications started to lose their effectiveness. Ruth had increasing pain, shortness of breath, and respiratory congestion, but the hospice team managed these symptoms. As Ruth was nearing death, the pastor, elders, deacons, and many from the congregation came to visit her. She lay peacefully in bed, singing the refrain from "It Is Well with My Soul" in a low, slightly gurgled voice. Eventually, with those she loved gathered around the room and the hospice nurse at her bedside, she fell silent as she became unresponsive, and a couple of hours later she fell peacefully asleep in the arms of Jesus. Youthful Ruth focused on spiritual restoration and the promise of future healing to come rather than the pursuit of physical healing to prolong her life in the here and now, and even though she refused cancer treatment and did not attempt to prolong her life, she glorified God.

The Christian's Compassionate Mission

Although all these principles are integrated, this fourth implication moves us outside the role of care receiver and into the role of compassionate caregiver. The Christian's mission in life parallels Jesus' mission, which was "to proclaim the year of the Lord's favor." We cannot redeem others by dying sacrificially on their behalf, nor do we possess special powers to perform healing miracles. Jesus was the unique, sacrificial Lamb that took away the sin of the world, and He was the Messiah whose healing touch, prayer, or spoken word removed sickness, eradicated disease, and raised the dead instantly. Only Jesus can reconcile people to God and bring them to human wholeness. This is what His redemption accomplished and the healing miracles He performed illustrated. Jesus does not want us to attempt to do these things either, but He certainly wants us to proclaim the year of the Lord's favor and show the same compassion He did. These two things must be at the heart of our use and application of medical science today.

Biblical compassion is characterized by a great affection or love for people in need, but it is not to be confused with sentimentalism (affections based solely on feelings without regard to truth). The Greek word for *compassion* used in the New Testament means literally "a fluttering heart of pity." Biblical compassion does not stop at the level of feelings, however, because it goes on to express those feelings in biblically defined practical works of mercy. There are two sides to compassion in the Bible: the first is a penetrating feeling of pity for those who are afflicted, and the second is the expression of pity in practical acts of mercy. Biblical compassion enters into the midst of others' suffering in order to share it with them and help them in wise, discerning, and caring ways.

In the story of the Good Samaritan (Luke 10:30–37), Jesus gives His clearest teaching on the core elements of biblical compassion, particularly toward a person in the midst of a medical crisis. Jesus spoke this parable after a Jewish religious official challenged Him. The religious official asked Jesus, "Who is my neighbor?" Jesus replied with this famous parable. The winding road from Jerusalem to Jericho was notorious for thieves. A poor, unsuspecting man, probably a Jew, was the victim of these rogues. He was beaten, robbed, stripped naked, and left half-dead on the side of the road. Two men passed by him—first a priest and later a Levite. If anyone should have shown compassion, it should have been one of these men of the cloth, but they were more concerned with their ritual purity (cf. Lev. 21:11) than with a naked, half-dead person on the side of the road, so they avoided him. Jesus identified a despised Samaritan (cf. John 4:9) as the compassionate hero who stopped, interrupted his business, rolled up his sleeves, and had a fluttering heart of pity for the man.

Jesus is teaching primarily that all people, even our enemies, are our neighbors, and we need to show compassion to all (Luke 6:27). Our hearts should go out to anyone who is afflicted, and we should exercise practical acts of mercy toward those we can help in our spheres of influence. As we seek to apply this to our mission to proclaim the year of the Lord's favor, we are engaged at once in a mission of mercy that is gospel-centered and universal in scope, divorced from any goal other than the satisfaction of showing the same compassion and proclaiming the same hope Jesus did.

Jesus teaches at least seven elements of biblical compassion in this story.

1. Biblical compassion will put other people's needs before our own. The Samaritan interrupted his schedule to help the injured man, and he responded to him in mercy with no questions asked.

2. Biblical compassion does not discriminate against race, creed, economic status, or color. It did not matter to the Samaritan if the man was a Jew. He saw a man in need, so he helped him.

3. Biblical compassion will take risks in order to help others. The Samaritan willingly risked his own safety—he could have been beaten and robbed.

4. Biblical compassion will seek to tend wounds, provide comfort, and alleviate pain and suffering. The Samaritan bandaged the man's wounds and applied oil and wine.

5. Biblical compassion will seek the comfort and safety of others. The Samaritan did not merely tend the wounds of the man and leave him; rather, he provided for his safety and welfare. He lifted him up, placed him on his animal, and brought him to a safe and comfortable place.

6. Biblical compassion will provide for the extended-care needs of others. The Samaritan brought the man to an inn, possibly a place that was skilled in nursing care, and paid for his stay with two

denarii, which would have covered two months'
room and board.

7. Biblical compassion follows up. The Samaritan
said he would return to check on the man after
he completed his business and pay for any additional expenses.

Jesus instructs us to live out these seven facets of compassion as we proclaim the year of the Lord's favor.

In summary, the principles we draw from Jesus'
teaching reveal an approach to medical care that is compassionate and redemptive in focus, where life and death
are not central, but the will of God is. In this model of
care, personal involvement, treating symptoms with
appropriate medical care that may or may not lead to a
cure, providing comfort, ensuring safety, and alleviating
pain and suffering are primary. Compassionate health
care seeks to promote the restoration of human wholeness that is spiritual in nature at present and physical
in the future, and it recognizes the limits of trying to
eradicate illness and disease through human intervention here and now. The timeless teaching of Scripture
has always been that there is hope and healing in Jesus
Christ, not in Asclepius, medical science, and certainly
not modern medicine, a topic we will turn to next.

Chapter 2

The Science of Hope

I have borrowed the title of this chapter from a University of Florida Health System (UF & Shands) slogan that describes its mission: "We're not only teaching tomorrow's physicians," according to the institution, "we're bringing new treatments, new advances, and new hope to patients sooner." The mission of UF & Shands is no different from any other hospital in the United States, which is to treat the sick, save lives, find new cures, and give people hope to live on in the here and now. In the little corner of northeast Florida where I live, along Interstate 95, billboard after billboard advertises medical institutions that promise the latest and greatest medical and surgical treatments to heal the injured, diseased, suffering, aging, and dying. Hospitals nationwide have become the institutions for hope and healing in the United States, but many Americans refuse to face the limit to the healing and hope these institutions offer.

Most advances in medical science positively influence the United States. Most, if not all, of us will experience an illness, disease, or injury that less than a hundred years ago would have been fatal. We receive immunizations to protect us from a whole host of invisible viruses and preventive medical instructions to steer us away from unhealthy life practices. We get diagnostic procedures galore—blood tests, X-rays, MRIs, CT scans, electrocardiograms—that reveal underlying disease and trauma that doctors can then treat effectively. Physicians prescribe a plethora of medications to eradicate infections, manage blood pressure, regulate diabetes, reduce anxiety, and treat many other conditions, and these medications enhance and prolong our lives. We have surgeries to remove diseased organs, bypass arteries, set bones, and deliver babies from complicated pregnancies. Indeed, advances in medical science are a real blessing.

The most recent advance on the American health-care landscape is the Affordable Care Act (ACA), popularly known as Obamacare. Although people in the health-care field have received the ACA with mixed emotions, the American population will now have unlimited access to the science of hope. President Barack Obama signed the ACA into law on March 23, 2010, and some of its initiatives are already in place, such as a free yearly health screening for Medicare recipients. The more sweeping changes will come in 2014, when the entire nation will be required to have health coverage under a government policy or private health plan or pay fines.

There have been recent legal challenges to the ACA, but in June 2012 the Supreme Court upheld the Act as constitutional. Undoubtedly, as the program unfolds, additional legal challenges will come, but for now Obamacare is here to stay, and the government will exercise more control over the science of hope and provide greater access to it for the American citizen. That the government would involve itself in regulating health care is a powerful testimony to the impact and effectiveness of medical science in the United States to combat disease, improve quality of life, and provide hope for people to live on in the here and now.

Before Modern Medical Science

People have not always had the quality of and accessibility to health care we have today. Poor hygiene, the improper disposal of human waste, and poor diet were common causes of illness, disease, and death in the past. On the streets of ancient European cities, human and animal excrement filled exposed side gutters. These fly-and-maggot-infested reservoirs harbored thousands of murderous microorganisms. Rats ran rampant in these cities, carrying parasites of infectious doom from place to place. The dreaded Black Plague meant certain death when it invaded a village or city. Scurvy, a condition easily reversible by ingesting vitamin C, ensured a slow, lingering death for sailors. Painful kidney stones and gout, caused by elevated amounts of uric acid in the body, were commonplace among those who drank excessive amounts of beer and wine and ate red meat—dietary staples until the nineteenth century. Rickets, a softening of the bones due to a lack of vitamin D, irreversibly deformed the bones of many unfortunate children. These and many more preventable causes of illness, disease, and death are reminders of how advances in medical science help us.

Early death was such a common occurrence that a body of literature arose called the *ars moriendi* (art of dying). These practical guides recommended prayers, gave counsel, and suggested attitudes and actions to ensure a good death and eternal life. Roman Catholics and Protestants alike contributed to this body of literature, with books such as *Preparation for Death* by the Christian humanist Erasmus (1466–1536); *The Art of Dying Well* by Cardinal Robert Bellarmine (1542–1641); and *A Salve for the Sick Man* by English Puritan William Perkins (1558–1602). Premature death occurred frequently in earlier times, and it was often a welcome reprieve from the suffering caused by the well-meaning quackery of a doctor and the bleeding of a barber (surgeon).

From the time Jesus healed the woman with a bleeding disorder who "suffered many things from many physicians" (Mark 5:26), not much changed in medicine for many centuries. Medical science was a relatively stagnant field until the rise of empiricism in the seventeenth century. In the late seventeenth century, Francis Bacon's (1561–1626) *New Organon* challenged the traditional ideas medicine embraced, and with this challenge a shift toward a more objective and analytical approach to the body, disease, and healing followed.

With Bacon, medical science established its footing firmly in naturalism, settling first for the naturalistic method reminiscent of Hippocrates (empiricism), but eventually moving in the direction of ontological naturalism (also called materialism or monism). In the naturalist mindset, immaterial entities do not exist; only tangible things do. Increasingly, as more "enlightened" scientists embraced materialism, they jettisoned anything and anyone that seemed supernatural, and human beings took center stage. Indeed, humans had become "the measure of all things," as the pre-Socratic philosopher Protagoras (490–420 BC) once said. As naturalists increasingly shunned the biblical account of creation, they needed to find a new story for the genesis of our existence. Charles Darwin's (1809–1882) theory of evolution filled the void. The idea that humans evolved from a random coagulation of primordial substance, through a variety of species, would have been laughable to Bacon, but it was his *New Organon* that sparked the scientific age and set medical science on the antibiblical footing of naturalism, humanism, and evolution.

The Baconian revolution was slow to evolve, however. During the seventeenth century and up into the nineteenth, speculative theories about disease still prevailed, and medical, pharmaceutical, and surgical care for the most part was still largely ineffective. In his essay "Medicine in Early Modern Europe, 1500–1700," from *The Western Medical Tradition: 800 BC to AD 1800,* Andrew Wear indicates that in the seventeenth century, out of every thousand live births up to two hundred infants died. During the same century, infectious disease killed 40 to 50 percent of children before the age of fifteen. The mean age for survival was fifty-five. These statistics do not change significantly until well into the twentieth century, with the advent of modern medical science.

The marriage between empiricism and technology gave birth to medical science as we know it today. In the late nineteenth century, Joseph Lister (1827–1912) developed his antiseptic technique in surgery after careful analysis of postoperative infections. The work of

Louis Pasteur (1822–1895) and Robert Koch (1843–1910) influenced Lister. These two men used a microscope to identify infectious microorganisms never seen before. In 1953 James Watson and Francis Crick identified DNA, the building blocks to biological life. These advancements, and many others in anatomy, physiology, microbiology, pharmacology, and biomechanical engineering, sent medical science on a rocket ride of change. In the twentieth century a paradigm shift took place in the world of medicine, now firmly rooted in naturalism, humanism, and evolution, which transformed the face of health care. This transformation changed the way doctors, surgeons, nurses, and pharmacologists understood the human body and disease, the way they practiced, and the way they were educated and trained. All this occurred in less than a century, and today new discoveries, treatments, and technologies are evidence of these dramatic advancements.

Some of these advancements have brought positive benefits, resulting in lives saved that in previous centuries would have been lost. In advanced trauma centers, patients may arrive in critical condition and near death, but experts in this area use cutting-edge technology to treat quickly and skillfully these seriously injured people and often save their lives. Technologies such as electrocardiograms, defibrillators, and pacemakers in the cardiac electrophysiology field extend lives. Alexander Fleming's 1928 discovery of penicillin, something we tend to take for granted today, has saved countless lives by halting the infectious process that, in centuries past, led to chronic conditions and death.

Since the relatively recent year 1975, medical science has made progress in the treatment of cancer, the leading cause of death for people under age sixty-five, and other disease conditions, and this has prolonged life considerably. According to the most recent statistics from the Center for Disease Control (CDC), cancer accounted for 574,743 of the 2,468,435 deaths in the United States in 2010. Because of advances in education, early detection diagnostics, chemotherapeutic agents, radiation treatments, surgery, and other state-of-the-art technology, the cancer victim's hope for survival has increased. The remaining 1,893,692 deaths would have occurred sooner, but advances in medical science delayed some of these deaths as well. The mean age for survival since the seventeenth century has increased from fifty-five to seventy-eight in the United States. The rate at which medical science has advanced in the past fifty years alone is phenomenal. There seems to be no end to the possibilities of medical science, the lives it can save, and the hope it can provide for those who are ill, diseased, injured, and dying, but it is crucial to remember that a hope built on faulty footing is a temporary hope at best.

Temporary Hope versus the Only Hope

As I noted in the introduction, the main reason I entered the health-care field was because I had an enthusiastic desire to provide people with hope to live on in the here and now. My thinking started to change, however, not about providing people with hope (this actually intensified), but about the way modern medicine presents itself as the hope for humankind. I struggled with the way modern medicine challenged Jesus and His healing hope, and how these temporary hopes have a tendency to lead people away from Him, just as the people in Pergamum went to Asclepius for healing and hope. Modern medicine has diverted hope away from Jesus in many ways and placed it squarely on itself. The science of hope the University of Florida Health System offers is clear testimony to this.

Accompanying the relatively recent rise of empirically based medical science in the United States has been a reversal in thought, even among some Christians. Faith-based hope took a back seat to the modern medical hope of living on in the here and now. When science broke free from the traditional ideas that hindered its advancement, people began to go to the opposite extreme by rejecting the Bible wholesale and putting agnosticism in its place. According to modern medicine, religion, or spirituality, is merely the handmaiden to the real hope medical science has to offer—the science of hope. Religious and spiritual beliefs may help you cope with your medical problems and provide a sense of hope when all else fails, but real hope is found in the healing that modern medical science provides *now*. This view is fundamentally agnostic, suggesting that we really don't know what is beyond the temporal, but if our faith in the unseen helps us cope in the real world presently, that is all that matters. The Bible is emphatically clear: Jesus' hope is not a mere handmaid to help people through a medical crisis, nor is He a hope to turn to after the science of hope fails. We would certainly expect this mindset to triumph outside the church, but the reality is it lurks in the church as well.

Several years ago, I was serving a congregation as its pastor, and one of the members suffered from an aggressive breast cancer. Karen's diagnosis was tragic, prognosis was grim, and treatment was futile. Nevertheless, Karen pursued the "hopeful" treatment options the oncologist offered.

"Pastor," she said, "next week I will have a mastectomy, and then I will start chemotherapy. I am going to beat this cancer! Pray that Jesus will pull me through." Then Karen did an about-face and left.

Karen sought no biblical counsel at all. She assumed God wanted her to pursue treatment to prolong her life, and she enthusiastically went after it. She did not return my calls, and several weeks later, she returned to church with a gaunt body, ghastly pale complexion, and a wig on her bald head. She wanted prayers only for getting well, and she talked constantly about how she was going to beat this cancer. Eventually she disappeared altogether, undoubtedly embracing the empty mantra to "live strong [and] find the cure." For her, Jesus was in the picture as a coping aide and miracle man to bring her physical healing, but her hope was really in modern medicine and its ability to cure her. She was trusting in the science of hope, not because she pursued treatment, but because she did not seek to understand her cancer in light of redemption, spiritual restoration, and human wholeness. In light of her eager pursuit, she also did not consider the most important realities behind the science of hope: treatment can be destructive, prolonging life may intensify suffering, and the hope it offers is limited.

Modern Medicine: Its Challenges and Limitations

In order to understand the limitations of the hope that modern medicine offers, we need to look more closely at some of the most common diseases people face today and the methods physicians often use to prolong life and achieve a cure.

Cancer

Cancer refers to renegade, out-of-control mutant cells that divide rapidly to form a localized mass of tissue, known as a tumor. As the mass grows and invades nearby tissues, organs, or bone, it may shed some of its cells. These cells may enter the blood stream or lymphatic system and travel to other parts of the body (metastasis). After a cancer diagnosis, the oncologist begins a process called staging. Staging determines the severity of the cancer, and it helps the oncologist develop a treatment plan. Common factors considered in staging are the location of the primary tumor site, the size and number of tumors in the body, and the spread of the cancer. Staging is a diagnostic process based on an oncologist's knowledge of how a particular cancer cell normally develops, how this type of cell typically spreads, and how deadly this type of cancer usually is.

Stage 0 cancer indicates a mass located in one part of the body with no metastasis. Stages 1, 2, and 3 cancers indicate a greater tumor size and invasion of a nearby organ, the blood stream, or the lymphatic system (the higher the number, the greater the severity). Stage 4 indicates cancer has spread to other parts of the body. Cancer staging is not an exact science, and it leaves room for interpretation. Nevertheless, it provides the most accurate information to date for an oncologist to determine diagnosis, course of treatment, and best guess for prognosis.

I have met people who had no treatment for cancer at all. Some of them lived on for several years, unexplainably defying the odds, and others died just as the doctor said they would. Physicians never really know with cancer, which is why it is so hard to treat. Cancer cells are "smart." They know how to mutate in order to become resistant to various chemotherapeutic agents, how to hide from diagnostic testing markers, how to start metastasizing, and how to go into remission. The reality: no one knows fully if pursuing treatment is the best option, especially when it is for cancer at an advanced stage.

Heart Disease
Cancer is an awful disease, but it is only one among many affecting the human race because of sin. For people over sixty-five, heart disease is the leading cause of death. According to the agency for National Health Statistics, heart disease is responsible for more than 25 percent of all deaths in America annually. In 2003, the *Journal of the American Medical Association* indicated that only 10 percent of the American population die suddenly (i.e., sudden heart attack); the remaining 90 percent die from chronic conditions such as heart disease, requiring long-term medical and surgical management. As a result, millions of people depend on modern medical intervention for each beat of their heart, and most of them are never prepared for the inevitable failure of modern medical techniques, nor are they prepared for the moral, ethical,

and economic quagmires that will come about as the span
of life increases due to state-of-the-art cardiac care.

Alzheimer's Dementia
Alzheimer's dementia was a relatively obscure disease,
but now with prolongation of life due to excellent cardiac care, it has become a household term. In 2009, the
Alzheimer's Association reported that over five mil-
lion Americans suffered from the disease. Alzheimer
and other types of dementias affect one in eight people
age sixty-five and older, and at age eighty-five, one out
of every two. Fifty to seventy percent of the residents
in nursing homes suffer from Alzheimer's disease and
related dementias. According to the Association, direct
and indirect costs relating to various types of dementia are more than $148 billion annually. The Federal
Agency on Aging reported that baby boomers (those
born between 1946 and 1964) started to turn sixty-five in
2011, and statistics indicate exponential growth of people
suffering from various dementias requiring long-term
nursing care. Modern medical science has very little in
its arsenal to treat these dementias, particularly in their
later stages. The sad reality for millions of these people
is that they will become dependents of the state in long-
term care nursing homes, and their children will forget
about them.

Modern Medicine: The Reality
Jack's experience is typical of how the philosophy of
modern medicine works out practically today. Jack
was diagnosed with hypertension and coronary artery

disease at fifty-six, and the doctor prescribed a blood pressure and cholesterol pill. At sixty-eight he retired, and shortly thereafter the doctor diagnosed him with low-grade prostate cancer. He had a radiation implant procedure to correct the problem. On his seventieth birthday, he had an episode of chest pain. He went to the hospital, and testing revealed four blocked coronary arteries. Jack had open-heart surgery. After the surgery, Jack developed a condition called ventricular tachycardia (fast heartbeat) and fibrillation, so he had an AICD placed in his chest. After a month, Jack was able to go home, but he had to return to the hospital for shortness of breath, which, as it turns out, was caused by congestive heart failure. Jack returned to the hospital repeatedly for the next few years with the same symptoms. At seventy-eight, Jack developed dementia. Six months after diagnosis he was unable to care for himself, so his family placed him in a nursing home. At eighty Jack was completely bed-bound and required total nursing care. The nursing staff crushed Jack's medications, all thirty of them, and put them in applesauce so he would take them. Jack went repeatedly via ambulance to the local hospital for aspiration pneumonia (liquid or food going into the lungs), and during his last visit the doctor surgically implanted a feeding tube in his abdomen. Now the nursing staff fed and administered his medications through the tube. At eighty-five Jack died, but only after the AICD repeatedly sent shocks through his heart in an effort to save his life. During his last days, Jack lay in an intensive care unit (ICU) connected to life support with no family at his bedside.

While this account may be exaggerated, it is not far from the actual experience of many people today. Although modern medicine may prolong life and provide hope to live on, the physical, psychological, social, and spiritual suffering it causes can be profound, never mind the financial burdens it produces, especially to Medicare. In 2010, the program *60 Minutes* aired "The Cost of Dying," an eye-opening investigative report on the cost of modern medicine to Medicare. The program reported that in 2009 Medicare "paid $50 billion just for doctor and hospital bills during the last two months of patients' lives—that's more than the budget for the Department of Homeland Security or the Department of Education." The report noted, among other things, that the daily average cost for a bed in an ICU is ten thousand dollars, and it estimated that 20 to 30 percent of the people treated in ICUs had no benefit from the care. The reality is the financial costs to Medicare will be unbearable in years to come, and future generations may not have Medicare to turn to for basic medical care. Dr. Ira Byock, a physician interviewed on the program, made an insightful observation: "Collectively, as a culture, we really have to acknowledge that we're mortal."

Another important reality is that medical science is merely the instrument, and it is the patient, the consumer, who drives it. The United States is a consumer-driven society, and this is no less true when it comes to health care, even presently under Obamacare, at least for now. In 1991, Congress passed the Patient Self-Determination Act (PSDA) to establish these rights. This act gives the competent adult the right to refuse or receive medical or surgical treatments and to make his own decisions regarding health care. Today, doctors provide opinions and options, but the patient decides how much treatment to receive. For better or worse, the patient (or health-care surrogate, if the patient is unresponsive or deemed incompetent) determines the course of treatment.

Several years ago I entered the field of hospice care. Hospice care is holistic care at end of life that manages pain, symptoms, suffering, and discomfort. It is a subspecialty in the health-care delivery system in the United States. Hospice care focuses on compassion, not prolongation of life, and some of its goals reflect the compassionate care model mentioned in the last chapter. A person enters a hospice program usually after a long, arduous battle with some disease accompanied by physical, mental, social, and spiritual pain, suffering, and upheaval. People are generally admitted to hospice when hope for a cure is no longer possible and death is on the horizon. It is the last stop in today's specialized health-care delivery system.

In some cases turned over to hospice care, the tension between the hope of modern medicine and the hope of Jesus becomes most shockingly apparent. With only a couple of weeks (sometimes hours) to live, patients are referred to hospice, unbearably suffering physically, psychologically, socially, spiritually, and completely void of hope. The medical science they have been trusting in has failed them, and they are not prepared for the failure. The science of hope promised them so much, but now reality hits—no more curative treatment, and no more hope.

Jim, an unfortunate patient I encountered through my work as a hospice nurse, also illustrates the harsh reality of modern medicine masquerading as hope. Sixty-year-old Jim suffered from lung cancer. It was on a hot day in July when I drove to his home to admit him to hospice. I knocked at the door, and his wife, who appeared very tense, answered. I introduced myself, and she escorted me up one flight of stairs to the living room, where Jim was sitting.

"Jim," his wife said, "this is Chris, the nurse from hospice."

I shook Jim's weak, trembling hand and proceeded as directed to sit on the couch. Jim's wife sat down on a chair across from me. Jim, with a bony face and sunken temples, oxygen prongs in his nose, and patches of hair growing back on his bald head, sat upright in a recliner. He was ashen in color and extremely thin, and the slightest movement caused him to be short of breath. The cancer and treatments had taken their costly toll on this once robust and healthy man, as the photographs around his house indicated.

I asked Jim and his wife what they knew about hospice care. Jim's wife said that it was for people who had exhausted all curative treatment options. I replied, "Yes, that is usually when people sign onto hospice. It is when the focus of care changes from pursuing a cure to seeking comfort." I looked over at Jim and asked him if he understood what I said.

He nodded yes and then went into a monologue about the cancer treatment he went through. He lost his breath as he spoke and had to pause repeatedly: "Two years ago I was diagnosed with lung cancer…I had one lung removed…started chemotherapy…the cancer did not go into remission…I sought treatment at a new cancer center…The cancer went into partial remission…not for long…more tests…treatments." Jim was extremely short of breath from talking, so he had to stop.

Jim's wife continued, "We depleted our life savings for the treatment because the insurance cap was reached, but the more treatment Jim received, the worse he got."

"Jim," I said, "it sounds like you've had quite a battle in such a short period of time. Are you ready to focus on staying home?"

His wife nodded yes, and Jim started to speak again: "It has been two years of misery."

"OK," I replied. Then I went on to explain the difference between hospice care and care to prolong life. "Hospice, as I mentioned already, is a type of care that does not seek to cure the disease. When people with cancer sign onto a hospice program, they are saying, in effect, 'I have had enough with seeking a cure.' This means no more diagnostic tests, chemotherapy, or other medical intervention to try to cure the cancer, but only medical management to treat the symptoms of the disease. The goal of hospice care is to provide you with support and comfort and to help you prepare for the days ahead. Do you understand what I just said?"

Jim sat quietly and contemplated what I said for about ten seconds before his wife looked over at him quizzically.

She said, "Jim, you are ready for hospice, right?"

Jim replied, "I have the CT scan on Tuesday."

Jim's wife became emotional and was obviously frustrated. "Jim, we discussed this already," his wife said tearfully. "Nothing more can be done, and the treatments are causing you to suffer. You can't even talk without becoming extremely short of breath, never mind going for the CT scan. Last night you nearly fell down when you got up to go to the bathroom, and you had a difficult time catching your breath. Jim, honey, nothing more can be done. Please sign onto hospice."

Jim looked over at me and said, "Can I still have the CT scan—while I am on the hospice program?"

I replied, "Normally when people sign onto hospice they are making a decision to forgo diagnostic procedures such as CT scans. Jim, I cannot decide for you either way, but I do share your wife's concern about your ability to go to the appointment. It is also important to remember that the doctor wanted us to talk to you. How about signing up for hospice today and signing off before going to the CT scan on Tuesday?"

Jim replied, "I just want to make sure—I'm not ready to give up..." before his wife interrupted.

She retorted in tears and frustration: "You just want to make sure? You don't want to give up? We have been trying to beat this for the past two years. Jim, you have exhausted all the treatment options; the doctors can't do anything else. You had several MRIs and CT scans. You had surgery, chemotherapy, and radiation. There is no more hope for a cure. Honey, I have been with you every step of the way. All this treatment has destroyed you and our lives, consumed our time, and depleted our finances. Even if the CT scan indicated the cancer was in full-blown remission, how is that going to change things now? You can barely talk and move! Please, Jim, please sign onto the hospice program. Let's try to make these final days as special as possible."

Jim nervously replied, "Sorry…honey, but I need to make sure…I have to make sure the cancer is incurable. The doctor said…that something new…a new drug… might come along."

We all sat quietly for a moment. Then I said to Jim, "You have a right to make that decision, and I will respect your choice, but I also think you will benefit from hospice, even if it is only for a few days."

Jim replied, "I want to wait."

I replied, "Is it OK if we call you after the CT scan?" Jim nodded yes.

I left my card and some information on the coffee table, arose from the couch, and shook Jim's hand. Jim's teary-eyed wife got up and escorted me down the stairs to the front door. We spent some additional time talking before I left.

Treatment Is Not Always the Best Option

Both Jack's and Jim's experiences show that there are times when treatment may actually do more harm than good. Not only is the science of hope shortsighted, its promises limited only to the here and now, but it may actually cause additional physical, mental, social, spiritual, and economic suffering. Through treatment, the physical body can be ravaged, the psyche dazed, a family ruined, financial security lost, and the hope of Christ diverted. In my years as a hospice nurse, I have seen Jim's situation repeatedly; sadly, I could replace Jim's name with many others.

Jim is one of countless Americans with cancer who was never prepared for the day treatment would become futile as the science of hope reached its limit. In order to promote an optimistic spirit, most treatment programs for cancer focus exclusively on hope in a cure, and this is what patients remember, even when reality is painting a different picture. These programs have treated many people successfully for less aggressive cancers, but the reality is cancer is still the leading cause of death for people under the age of sixty-five in the United States. According to the American Cancer Society, one out of every four people diagnosed with cancer dies. In its Cancer Trends Progress Report, the National Cancer Institute indicates that people diagnosed early with cancer who receive a positive prognosis and have treatment will still have a significant chance for recurrence in the future. These statistics do not foster an optimistic outlook for people suffering with cancer, but they are important to consider, especially as a patient considers treatment.

Treatment for cancer can sometimes be worse than the disease. Jim may have succeeded in prolonging his life, but it was at a great cost to his family and him. I have met several people who wished they never had treatment for their cancer because of the physical, emotional, social, and economic toll it took. Chemotherapy and radiation treatments can be absolutely miserable and expensive. The regime can cause nausea, vomiting, diarrhea, dehydration, extreme exhaustion, hair loss, burns, loss of appetite, problems with cognition (chemo brain), and infections because of a decreased immune system (opportunistic infections). Once patients begin treatment, their lives are consumed with diagnostic procedures, doctor appointments, and hospitalizations (sometimes due to complications from the treatment), and they sacrifice precious time with family, friends, and life in general. The reality is that aggressive curative treatment may not always be the best option. For some patients it leads to a false hope that is physically, emotionally, spiritually, socially, and financially draining—if not entirely destructive both temporally and eternally. Consider the example of Mary, who demonstrates that treatment can sometimes be more harmful than good.

Mary was a middle-aged married woman with two children (ages 17 and 14) who was diagnosed with advanced breast cancer. The cancer treatment wreaked havoc on Mary and her family. Mary's prognosis was three months without treatment, but perhaps longer if she had surgery, chemotherapy, and radiation treatments. Mary chose the treatment, which included a radical mastectomy followed by chemotherapy infusions and radiation treatments. The surgery went well with no complications, and a few days after the surgery, Mary went home to be cared for by home health services.

The week after the surgery, Mary started outpatient chemotherapy and radiation treatments. After the first month, Mary lost all her hair, and she was weak, tired, and nauseated most of the time. She also became bitter, resentful, and critical toward those close to her, particularly her husband and children. At three months, after two visits to the local emergency room (ER) for nausea, vomiting, and dehydration caused by the treatments, Mary had to return to the hospital. This time she had to stay because she suffered from anorexia, dehydration, and depression. During her hospital admission, the oncologist ordered a repeat scan, which revealed continued progression of the disease. He recommended another round of a different type of chemotherapy after stabilization. Mary consented to the treatment.

Due to her critical status, Mary had to remain in the hospital during these treatments. Four months after her diagnosis, Mary was unable to eat, so she required a feeding tube. At five months, Mary weighed eighty-five pounds and developed bedsores on her buttocks, suffered from excruciating pain, and was in a state of clinical depression. The visits from her family diminished to one time a week. Mary was in the hospital for two long months, but it appeared the new treatment was working, so the hospital transferred her to a rehabilitation center.

At the six-month mark, Mary started a rehabilitation program. The areas on her buttocks were not healing, however, and she continued to have excruciating pain in her upper back. A repeat scan revealed that the cancer had started to spread once again. The oncologist referred Mary to a hospice program. With all hopes dashed, Mary went home and reluctantly signed onto home hospice.

The physical, mental, and spiritual anguish Mary suffered from continued unabated. Everyone around her felt the misery she was going through. Her husband turned to alcohol to cope with the stress, and her children were having problems at school. At the end of eight months, even with the dedicated hospice staff, Mary died an awful death with great suffering. In the aftermath, her husband lost his job due to alcohol abuse, and, without an attentive parent to help them cope with their loss, both children ran away from home. In time, the police arrested the older child for possession of drugs, and the younger child committed suicide by jumping in front of a train. Mary lived five months longer with treatment—but at a great cost to her and her family. Treatment is not always the best option.

The Failure of the Science of Hope

As we have seen in this chapter, medical treatment is expensive, but aside from the costs for treatment is the incalculable cost of hopelessness to patients and families because the science of hope did not pay off as it promised. The ACA may open the way for all Americans to have health care, and the PSDA may put them in charge of it, but the science of hope is shortsighted and constrained to the here and now because it rests on the flimsy pillars of naturalism, humanism, agnosticism, and evolution. Today's medical consumer is seeking with all diligence to live on in this present life, but the reality is that he or she cannot. Christians should be at the forefront proclaiming this truth today, but some are trusting in the same faulty hopes—not necessarily out of a spirit of defiance, but because the field of modern medical science is highly technical and hard to understand. In the next chapter, we will consider how to navigate the complex world of modern medical science based on the compassionate care model presented in the first chapter.

Chapter 3

Medical Science:
Biblically Informed

I met Freddy in the fall of 2006. He was a seven-year-old boy referred to hospice because he was in a so-called persistent vegetative state (PVS) with no hope of recovery. While he had been visiting with his father, he had fallen off a dock and nearly drowned. Because of his father's prompt intervention and the quick response of the emergency medical service (EMS), his life was spared. After a month passed, though, Freddy was still unresponsive and connected to a ventilator. On the advice of Freddy's doctors, Sarah, Freddy's mother and custodial parent, made the decision to sign a DNR order and wean him off the ventilator. Remarkably, after withdrawing the apparatus, he breathed on his own, but he was still unresponsive. A battery of neurological exams and diagnostic tests followed, all of which confirmed chronic PVS.

Caring for Freddy

A pediatric palliative care team and my hospice collaborated to care for Freddy. The plan was for the team from the children's hospital and my home hospice agency to work closely together in the child's "end-of-life" care. I first met Freddy at a special-needs school he attended. He was sitting in a specialized wheelchair in a reclined position with eyes fixated. His eyes would shift from side to side occasionally and blink, and he would cough periodically. He was completely paralyzed, and he received feedings and medications through a tube inserted into his abdomen. I approached Freddy, stroked his head, held his flaccid hand, and spoke to him. He just sat— immobile. I performed my assessment and developed a plan of care. I would eventually visit with Freddy on three more occasions at his school. I noticed on my visits that it seemed as if Freddy's countenance lifted, his eyes flickered, and his respirations relaxed when I drew near. I knew Freddy had a soul, but I brushed off these findings as purely subjective on my part—that is, until I spoke to others involved in his daily care and reflected more deeply on what it means for someone to have a soul. The nursing staff at the school, his teacher, the hospice social worker, and Sarah reported the same experience. It appeared to all of us that something was going on inside Freddy, something that human contact could detect but sophisticated instrumentation and neurological examinations could not.

I suspected Freddy would develop pneumonia, which would be his demise. It was important to find out if Sarah was going to allow the use of antibiotics to treat the symptoms of pneumonia. What I did not know is that a conversation between the pediatric palliative care team and Sarah had already taken place a couple of weeks before my first visit with him. If Freddy developed pneumonia, we would not administer antibiotics, as this would be a curative rather than palliative measure. I was uncomfortable with this decision.

When I met with Sarah at her home, we discussed Freddy's case and the use of antibiotics. She said she had decided not to use the antibiotics based on the pediatric palliative care team's counsel, but she didn't know if she had made the right decision. It became apparent to me that Sarah was ambivalent. I reported these findings to the pediatric palliative care team and expressed my concerns about Sarah's ambivalence.

The pediatric palliative care team set the counsel they gave to Sarah in the following context: Freddy is in chronic PVS and has no quality of life. According to all the tests, there is no chance for recovery. Using antibiotics to treat the symptoms of pneumonia would be a curative and not a palliative measure. The concern is that Freddy's youthful body will bounce back from the pneumonia after the antibiotic treatment. This will only serve to prolong a life of suffering for Freddy, and it will not allow his young mother to move on with her life. I expressed my discomfort with and unwillingness to follow this plan to the pediatric palliative care team and my superiors.

My resistance to this plan stemmed from several factors. First, Sarah was ambivalent concerning the decision. She had several reasons for her ambivalence, as I later found out. Obviously, she was the child's mother. What sane mother wants her child to die? She was also very impressionable and in a state of conflict concerning her son's condition. Her desire was to trust the professionals, but something else was telling her to trust her feelings.

Underneath all of this, as I discovered later, was a Christian belief system that valued life simply for life's sake.

Second, the team made a judgment about Freddy's quality of life based on functionality. The ability of a person to perform certain activities in life does not indicate quality. Utilizing criteria is necessary to grade a person's ability to perform activities of daily living and interact with the environment, but they do not define quality of life. Although Freddy was difficult to care for, his mother, family, and friends found delight in caring for him, and Freddy appeared to appreciate it. The existence of life gives life quality, regardless of a person's functional state.

Third, testing used to diagnose Freddy assumed a monistic view of the human person, a philosophical idea, mentioned earlier, that says human beings are composed of one material substance. Monism rejects dualism, the belief that human beings possess a physical body and immaterial soul, which is what Christians believe. There were several people involved in Freddy's daily care who believed there was something going on inside him, regardless of what the sophisticated equipment and neurological exams reported. Neurological testing and diagnostic apparatus can provide information about a person's neuronal activity, the brain's anatomy and physiology, and spinal cord function, but they provide us with very little data when it comes to a person's conscious or unconscious state. Only an individual can truly determine his own conscious state because he has privileged accessed to it.

Unresponsiveness and Consciousness

Dr. Daniel Robinson, distinguished professor emeritus of philosophy and psychology at Georgetown University whose professional expertise is in the field of neuropsychology, highlights the complexity of attempting to detect consciousness in unresponsive people. Robinson's lectures, "Consciousness and Its Implications," provide important insights. Robinson mentions Terry Wallis, a man who was in an unresponsive state and awoke after nineteen years. Remarkably, new nerve tissue developed in areas of Wallis's brain unaffected by his injury. Patricia Bull, an unresponsive patient in New Mexico, awoke after sixteen years. One day she unexpectedly told a shocked nurse to leave her bedding alone. Brian Cressler, a young man involved in a motor vehicle accident, was in an unresponsive state for a year-and-a-half before he awoke. A young woman named Judy was in an unresponsive state for three months. Surprisingly, after she woke up she expressed frustration toward her attending physician, who told his residents and interns repeatedly that she would never wake up! In fact, many have emerged from unresponsive states and resumed lives not unlike the ones they had left behind.

Karen Ann Quinlan was in so-called PVS, yet her EEG readings showed normal electrical activity in her brain.[1] A study conducted on forty patients in PVS

---

1. Karen Ann Quinlan (1954–1985) was an important figure in the right-to-die controversy in the United States. In 1975, Quinlan fell unconscious and slipped into a coma. After she had been on life support for several months, her parents asked the hospital to discontinue active care and allow her to die. Legal battles ensued, and in 1976, the New Jersey Supreme Court

found that seventeen were misdiagnosed, and thirteen of the participants showed signs of recovery during the trial period. This indicates that considerable skill and long-term analysis are required to diagnose PVS, says Robinson, if a diagnosis of PVS is even possible. Dr. Stephen Nelson, the neuropathologist who performed the late Terri Schiavo's[2] autopsy, wrote these revealing words on page 20 of his report to the Tenth Judicial Circuit Court in Florida: "The decedent's brain—or any brain for that matter—cannot prove or disprove a diagnosis of persistent vegetative state."

Factors in Treating Freddy

In Freddy's case, it was necessary to consider several important factors. First, Dr. Robinson notes that a psychological state is subjective, and an outsider's access to it is privileged. When we are sleeping, we have numerous sensations, and we may be self-consciously aware of some of those sensations in dreams. If we do not dream, however, we have no subjective awareness at all. Nevertheless, we do not consider ourselves to be in a persistent vegetative state. We protect a person who is sleeping because

---

ruled in her parents' favor. Disconnected from life support, Quinlan lived on for ten more years before dying of pneumonia in 1985.

2. Another legal battle over the issue of discontinuing life support revolved around Terri Schiavo (1963–2005). Schiavo collapsed in her home in 1990 and went into full cardiac arrest; after being in a coma for two-and-a-half months she was diagnosed with PVS. Her husband, Michael, wished to have her feeding tube removed, but Schiavo's parents argued that she was still conscious. Despite the eventual involvement of the federal government, with President George W. Bush signing legislation to keep Schiavo alive, the federal court system upheld the original court's decision to remove the feeding tube. It was removed on March 18, 2005, and Schiavo died on March 31, 2005.

we believe he or she will wake up; we need to extend the same courtesy to those in an unresponsive state.

Second, young children in an unresponsive state have a greater chance for recovery, even years later. Therefore, rehabilitative and maintenance regimes should be in place for children with PVS.

Third, the criteria used to define *brain death* are controversial. The definition, found in the Uniform Definition of Death Act (UDDA), includes irreversible cessation of all brain functions as determined by instrumentation, neurological assessment, and subjective opinion. The people mentioned here simply do not fit the criteria, not even the late Terri Schiavo, who was starved to death, and surely not young Freddy.

Fourth, the team was going to withhold antibiotic treatment to prevent a life of suffering for Freddy. At the end of life, hospices treat symptoms caused by an infection in one of two ways. The first is by administering antibiotics. This avenue of treatment may palliate the symptoms, but it may cause uncomfortable side effects, produce resistant strains of bacteria that potentially may be harmful to others, and, in the end, prolong life. The second option is to withhold antibiotics. If hospices choose this avenue, other medications palliate the symptoms, and the person eventually experiences sepsis and dies. In the elderly population, withholding antibiotics may be appropriate under certain circumstances, but in the younger population, withholding antibiotics may not be the best avenue for palliation of symptoms. Antibiotics are the most effective way to treat symptoms and provide comfort among those in the pediatric population who have infections, and they are in keeping with biblical compassion, which is an exercise of love respecting the will of God concerning life and managing suffering that does not cause harm to others (Rom. 13:10).

Fifth, the team said that keeping Freddy alive would not allow his mother to move on with her life, counsel that was based on purely self-serving motives. Freddy's mother was encouraged to think about attending a college and pursuing a career in anticipation of her son's death! This counsel was extremely confusing to her. Christians serve others, not themselves, and Freddy's mother wanted to serve her son, regardless of his condition.

My superiors encouraged me to revisit Sarah and develop a plan of care that would help settle her ambivalence, and, after this meeting, we would all meet together and establish a revised plan of care. If Sarah desired to withhold the antibiotics, my superiors would reassign the case to respect my convictions.

Sarah greeted me at the door: "Come in, Chris. I have to finish with Freddy's morning feeding." She briskly walked from the front door to Freddy's room, and I followed.

"How is Freddy doing?" I asked.

"He had a lot of visitors yesterday. His aunt stopped by, and some friends from church visited." His mother went to work on the abdominal tube.

I looked over at Freddy lying in bed, dressed in his pajamas, clean, well kept, soundless, and immobile. His mother skillfully opened the tube, injected his anti-seizure medication, and started the feeding. Sarah was proficient with his care and required no instruction. I went on to perform my assessment of Freddy.

After my examination, I looked over at the wall across from the bed and noticed a clipping from a newspaper. It was a picture of Freddy, with a big smile, playing with other children just before the drowning accident. I walked over and took a closer look. The article was about a school Freddy attended. Sarah reminisced about the picture, remembering her once-energetic son. I saw a Bible on the windowsill, and I asked Sarah if she read to him. "Yes, every night," she replied.

After she was done with Freddy's care, we sat down in the living room, and I commented on how well Sarah cared for Freddy. Sarah admitted that it was difficult, but, becoming tearful, she said that it meant a lot to her. She began crying as she went on to say, "I know it means a lot to Freddy too." I agreed that I believed her care meant a lot to Freddy, but I told her that it also meant a lot to God. I reminded her that in the story of the Good Samaritan, the man who showed compassion for the injured man was the one who pleased God. I told her, "Your care for Freddy does not go unnoticed by him, God, or your friends."

I then discussed the use of antibiotics and reported that on my exam I noticed slight congestion in Freddy's chest. "Freddy may develop pneumonia soon," I said. "It is important to know your wishes concerning the antibiotics." She asked me what I would do in her situation, and I told her I would use liquid antibiotics (rather than intravenous) through Freddy's abdominal tube to treat the pneumonia. I explained that eventually the antibiotics would lose their effectiveness, and when that happened, we would know it was God's will to take Freddy. "But right now," I said, "I think it is important to use the antibiotics." Sarah relaxed and agreed that she liked my proposed plan.

Sarah was present at our team discussion two days later when the pediatric palliative care team accused me of imposing my beliefs on her and causing her confusion. I explained that we shared the same beliefs and she had asked for my opinion, so I had given it. During the meeting, the team asked Sarah about using antibiotics. Without hesitation, she said that if Freddy developed pneumonia she wanted to use antibiotics through the tube to manage his symptoms.

As expected, Freddy developed pneumonia a week later, and he received antibiotics via his abdominal tube. In addition, as anticipated, the congestive and feverish symptoms of his pneumonia were treated, and he lived on. Two months after this bout of pneumonia, I discharged Freddy from our hospice program, and the hospice social worker enrolled him in a special program that provided rehabilitative care and support for children with Freddy's condition. Freddy went on to live in a so-called persistent vegetative state, exuding a brightness when certain people drew near, both of these observations based purely on subjective experience and personal beliefs—not science.

Modern Medical Assumptions versus Biblical Assumptions

Modern medicine is not medical science, as we noted in the last chapter. It is a philosophy of care based on ontological naturalism (monism or materialism), evolutionary biology, and humanistic psychology. As we saw in the case of Freddy, the assumptions of modern medicine directed the care, advice, morals, and ethics of the health-care professionals and institutions involved in his care. It is important for us to be aware of this so that well-meaning health-care professionals who do not share our beliefs will not lead us astray. It is equally important for us to understand clearly how the Bible views illness, disease, life, and death so that we will make biblically informed medical decisions that honor God. Medical science does not exist in a vacuum, and the Bible is sufficient to fill the philosophical void it requires.

There are three basic assumptions modern medicine possesses about illness, disease, life, and death. First is a belief that the human person consists of one substance—an idea called monism, materialism, or ontological naturalism. In modern medical terminology, the words *spirit*, *soul*, and *mind* may be used, but in practice, modern medicine holds to a naturalistic and evolutionary view of the human person that is materialistic in orientation. This presupposition shapes the criteria used to define *brain death*, which assumes that a lack of electrical activity in the brain equals a brain that is dead. We will study this subject at length later. A second assumption is a belief that we evolved from lower forms to higher forms of life—evolution. Progress, survival, and functionality define who we are as individuals and are indicators of whether the life we live has quality. In an evolutionary context, life is lived between the points of viability and utility. The third assumption is a belief that we are inherently good, and humans are at the center of the world. Human sinfulness is not the problem that plagues us;

illness, disease, and death are, and the goal of modern medicine is to eradicate these evils and do everything in its power to accommodate the intrinsic human need for hope to live on in this life until a person is no longer functional. These are the three main assumptions undergirding modern medicine and its practice today.

At the core of the tension between modern medicine and a biblical view of medical science is the former's denial of the Bible's sufficiency and necessity for life and practice. Put simply, Christians affirm the absolute truth claims of Holy Scripture, and health-care professionals indoctrinated by modern medicine do not. Therefore, Christianity takes a radically different stance toward illness, disease, life, and death. First, Christianity assumes the human person is dualistic in nature; we possess material bodies and immaterial souls (Gen. 2:7). This means that if a person is diagnosed brain-dead or in a persistent vegetative state but is still able to breathe without artificial life support, he or she is still living, even if diagnostic testing indicates no brain activity. Second, God made the first human beings, so-called *Homo sapiens*, through a one-time deliberate act of creation (Gen. 1:27). Progress, survival, and functionality do not define a person's quality of life; rather, the fact a person is living gives life quality. Third, sin plunged the entire human race into a state of misery, and Jesus provides the only way of escape (Acts 4:12; Rom. 5:12). Illness, disease, and death are not the root problems but rather the symptoms; the real problem is sin. Jesus Christ provides spiritual healing from sin in the present and the hope for physical healing in the future, but only those who have put Him at the center of their life and world are able to accept this truth. On these vital matters, Christianity rests on vastly different assumptions from modern medicine; therefore, it is crucial for Christians to understand these differences so that their medical decisions will be biblically informed.

A Biblical Response to Modern Medical Dilemmas

Today, when people face an emergency similar to Freddy's, they find themselves in the midst of modern medical science's highly technical world. A family member has a cardiopulmonary arrest, which means his heart and lungs do not work effectively to sustain life due to an illness, disease process, or trauma, and EMS arrives on the scene. The highly trained EMS staff initiates basic and advanced cardiac life support and transports the person quickly to a local emergency room. By the time the person arrives at the ER, his heart has been shocked to restart it (defibrillated), intravenous medications have been administered, and an artificial breathing tube has been inserted (intubated) into his mouth and trachea (windpipe). At the ER, resuscitation continues until stabilization, and then the patient is whisked off to an ICU on a ventilator. As hours and days in the ICU pass, several dilemmas arise that require biblically informed decisions.

In this section, we will consider a biblical approach to some of the dilemmas that arise in the critical and intensive care hospital setting. It is important to keep in mind that the counsel given here is not exhaustive and that there are no one-size-fits-all answers. These are only general principles that we hope will provide helpful guidance for individual situations.

Dilemma 1: If the initial act of resuscitation did not occur quickly, there will be little hope for unimpaired survival. At the onset of a cardiopulmonary arrest, a person becomes nonresponsive within several seconds, and measurable brain activity will cease twenty to forty seconds later. If the organs do not receive oxygenated blood, ischemic injury from the deficient supply of blood, resulting in decreased oxygen, occurs. The brain suffers injury the quickest due to ischemia (deficient supply of blood to a body part). In the ICU, diagnostic testing will occur, and the data gathered from these tests will help to determine prognosis.

At this point, four major issues concern the Christian. First, a declaration of brain death may occur. If a person is determined to be brain-dead, legally he or she is considered dead, even if the life-support apparatus is still connected. Second, the testing used to determine the level of consciousness in unresponsive people—and, therefore, brain death—is highly subjective and based upon a strictly monistic view of the human person. Third, organ donors pronounced legally dead might have their organs harvested before they have been completely removed from life support. Fourth, the question ultimately arises for family members: Is it acceptable to take my loved one off life support?

A declaration of brain death based on the medical community's definition of life and death today poses significant challenges for Christians. Before the middle of the twentieth century, the medical community defined death as the absence of cardiac and respiratory function. In the 1960s, however, advancements made it increasingly possible to reverse cardiac and respiratory arrest by cardiopulmonary resuscitation (CPR), defibrillation, mechanical ventilation, medications, and other treatments. Now, cardiac arrest and respiratory failure do not define death; rather, a person who suffers cardiac arrest and respiratory failure is in a state called *clinical death.* Technological advances have enabled the medical community to reverse the state of clinical death and maintain life, but often at the expense of brain function. As a response to the ability to resuscitate individuals and keep them alive mechanically, *brain death* has now emerged as a legal definition of death.

Biblically defined, a person is dead when the heart and lungs have ceased to function (Job 27:3; Ps. 104:29; Mark 15:37). If a person has no breathing and no heartbeat, he will not have brain function, and at this point, he may be declared dead. This means that if a person on artificial life support is determined to be brain-dead, it will be necessary to withdraw the life-support apparatus completely to see if he is truly dead. If the heart and lungs function after the apparatus is withdrawn, then the person is not dead, even if the so-called brain-dead condition persists and even if sophisticated diagnostic equipment and a team of expert neurologists declare the condition irreversible. Because the legal definition of *brain death* does not match the biblical definition of death, Christians cannot ethically consider a person who is declared brain-dead to be truly dead.

Second, the testing used to determine brain death is highly subjective and assumes a monistic view of man. Christians affirm a dualistic (body/soul union), as opposed to a monistic (body only), view of the human person. Genesis 2:7 says, "The LORD God formed man of the dust of the ground [body], and breathed into his nostrils the breath of life [life force or soul]; and man became a living being [human person]." Data gained from neurological testing are extremely helpful to understand what is going on in the physical body, but they provide no information about the condition of the soul in an unresponsive person. As I have explained, death occurs biblically when the heart and lungs cease to function on their own. The absence of neurological activity in the brain indicates only a lack of neurological activity in the brain, but not necessarily a lack of psychological or spiritual activity and certainly not the absence of life.

Third, brain-dead organ donors are legally dead; thus, their organs may be removed legally while their heart is still beating. This practice happens often today. In 1981, a presidential commission issued a report called *Defining Death: Medical, Legal, and Ethical Issues in the Determination of Death.* This report is the basis for the UDDA, which is law in nearly all fifty states. Using brain-death criteria, a person may be declared legally dead while his heart is still beating and before life support has been completely withdrawn. With the support of this act, some medical institutions harvest organs from these people. Procuring organs may actually be their cause of death, so this is an unethical practice for Christians (Ex. 20:13; Rom. 13:10).

Fourth, is it acceptable to withdraw life support? If a person is connected to cardiopulmonary life support, it is not wrong to remove it, but those who are making this decision should recognize that several factors are involved and a great deal of medical and biblical wisdom is required in making this decision. In the end, God determines when a person lives or dies, not the life-support apparatus (Eccl. 3:2). It is also important to remember that many of the life-support options available today were not available less than a hundred years ago. As noted in the first chapter, the Bible requires compassionate care, not aggressive curative intervention to prolong life at all costs. In most cases, eventually it will be necessary to remove cardiopulmonary life support to determine if an unresponsive person is truly dead. Again, cessation of heart and lung function determines death biblically, not unresponsiveness and a diagnosis of brain death.

Dilemma 2: The longer a person is in the ICU on life support, the greater the number of decisions his caregivers will have to make. These decisions have very little to do with medical science, but they have everything to do with beliefs and values. In recognition of this, Congress enacted the PSDA, which I mentioned briefly in the last chapter. The patient, or health-care surrogate in the case of unresponsive or confused individuals, has three rights: (1) the right to participate in and direct health-care decisions; (2) the right to accept or refuse medical or surgical treatment; and (3) the right to prepare advance medical directives (DNR orders and living wills). Doctors offer options, give opinions, and provide guidance, but it is ultimately the patient or health-care surrogate who makes these difficult decisions. Again, the longer an unresponsive person is on life support in the ICU, the more numerous, complex, and multifaceted these decisions will become.

If a person has a poor prognosis, the doctor should suggest a DNR order. A DNR order will prevent heroic life-saving measures from occurring if the person has a subsequent cardiac or respiratory arrest. It is an order the doctor writes in collaboration with a patient (if responsive and competent) or health-care surrogate. The doctor should explain the diagnosis and prognosis and give his opinion about whether he believes a DNR order is appropriate. It is important to remember the doctor is giving an opinion, so there is nothing wrong with asking for a second opinion.

As time passes for the patient in the ICU, it will be necessary to remove the breathing tube from his mouth and perform a procedure called a tracheotomy. During this surgical procedure, the doctor makes an incision in the trachea in order to establish an airway, and he inserts a plastic tube through the site. This, rather than the mouth, will be the new breathing site for the patient. Before performing this procedure, however, the removal of the old breathing tube will need to occur, so there will be the option to remove the ventilator entirely, provided the person has a DNR order. Depending on prognosis, a tracheotomy may not be the best option because it may cause a person more suffering and harm. Sometimes it is better for the health-care surrogate to sign a DNR order, remove the breathing tube, and keep the person comfortable with medications such as morphine. Whether the person lives or dies rests in the hands of God.

In the ICU, the kidneys may become impaired and stop working for any number of reasons. The kidneys filter impurities from the blood, and if they are not properly functioning, toxins will build up in the body and eventually death will result. A procedure called dialysis corrects this problem. During dialysis, a catheter diverts blood from the body to a machine for filtration. After the machine cleans the blood, it circulates it back to the body. Again, depending on prognosis, dialysis may not be the best option to pursue because it may only serve to increase suffering and prolong an imminent death.

Eventually, the original feeding tube, which goes either through the nose or mouth to the stomach, will need to be replaced by a tube in the abdomen—the infamous feeding tube. This procedure is invasive as well. It requires an incision through the abdominal wall into the gastrointestinal tract and the insertion of a small rubber hose. The insertion of an abdominal feeding tube is required following a tracheotomy, and it usually occurs after a long stay in the ICU that is heading toward a chronic-care situation. We will look at feeding tubes in detail in our discussion of the third dilemma, which addresses chronic conditions.

In summary, it is important to remember the longer a person is unresponsive in the ICU, the less the chance for unimpaired recovery and the greater the potential for complications requiring further aggressive, invasive, and expensive treatment. At each step of the way, difficult decisions concerning life and death are required, and it is not easy to give rigid principles for clear guidance. Each case is unique, so it is important to listen carefully to the professionals, remembering that their underlying assumptions may not be biblically informed. In the midst of all the complexities, however, it is important to remember that the curative options to prolong life may not be the most compassionate choices Jesus requires of us. He does not mandate aggressive treatment to prolong life at all costs, but He requires compassionate care informed by the principles we draw from the concept of the year of the Lord's favor. It is also crucial to remember that less than seventy years ago, many of these treatments did not even exist! Withdrawing life support is not necessarily a sin; in fact, it may be the most biblical choice, especially if a protracted stay in the ICU is motivated by idolatrous hopes of prolonging life rather than God's prescriptive will and His glory.

Dilemma 3: There are times when people will run through the whole series of procedures in the ICU and pull through, but will remain unresponsive. These people are taken off the life-support apparatus and their heart and lungs function independently, but now they are breathing through a tracheostomy (or not), are fed through an abdominal tube, and require long-term nursing care. These individuals, like young Freddy, are in so-called PVS. There are also other long-term care conditions, such as Alzheimer's disease, Parkinson's disease, dementia, cerebral vascular accident (CVA or stroke), and degenerative neurological conditions (MS and ALS), that give rise to similar chronic-care decisions.

The first issue to consider is the pursuit of aggressive curative treatment in the future. This may be in the form of any medical or surgical intervention that seeks to cure a future life-threatening condition. For example, an eighty-year-old woman with Alzheimer's disease develops breast cancer. It would not be compassionate for her caregivers to pursue aggressive curative treatment for the cancer because it will only serve to increase her suffering. Even if the treatment regime, which would undoubtedly traumatize the poor, confused woman, cured the cancer, the Alzheimer's disease would not improve. Again, there is nothing wrong with refusing curative treatment when it will only prolong suffering. It is also a good idea to have a DNR order in place when a condition is chronic and degenerative in nature and prognosis is poor. This will mean health-care professionals will not be obligated to attempt heroic measures to resuscitate an individual with a terminal diagnosis.

Nutrition and hydration are always issues that arise with chronic health conditions. Christians have a moral and ethical obligation to provide food and drink to those in need (Matt. 25:44), but they are not required to feed people against their will (cf. Matt. 10:14). The difficulty arises because we possess ways to provide nutrition and hydration that did not exist a hundred years ago. Feeding tubes and various types of intravenous solutions allow us to feed and hydrate people, perhaps even against their will. It will be helpful to look at three scenarios and consider the Christian's response to each.

The first scenario is when a person has a feeding tube already in place. The person who is in an unresponsive state with a feeding tube already placed requires feeding. In such instances a moral and ethical precedent has been set (Job 1:21; 33:4). We need to remember, however, there are times when feeding people via a feeding tube may cause a fluid overload in the body. If this happens, it may impair heart and lung function and cause the person to suffer. In these cases, it may be necessary to draw back and eventually stop the feedings. The person in an unresponsive state with a feeding tube needs close monitoring, and he or she requires feeding until problems arise that cause suffering and possible death.

The second scenario is the person who has a medical condition that makes chewing and swallowing a problem. As good stewards, we should care for our bodies. If avenues exist for us to take in nutrition and hydration we should use them, provided they do not cause complications or intensify suffering (1 Cor. 3:16–17). The same principle stands for those who are unable to speak for themselves, unless they indicate otherwise in a living will (a document defining a person's health-care wishes that we will discuss later). When we were infants, some of us were fed through various technologies, such as a bottle and nipple; the same courtesy should extend to those who cannot speak for themselves but require a technological device, such as a feeding tube, to eat. Again, this feeding and hydration require close monitoring in unresponsive people and discontinuation when complications arise.

The third case is a person who is refusing to eat. If a young person is refusing to eat and drink, he or she is usually depressed. The same may be true for older people. In such cases, once the underlying condition of depression is treated, the person starts to eat. There are times, however, when elderly people, even those who are chronically confused, are not depressed and simply refuse to eat, a condition called adult failure to thrive. These people are making a conscious choice not to eat, perhaps because they are dying (Eccl. 12:3). Their weak and debilitated bodies cannot handle food and hydration, so they are choosing not to eat and drink. It is important not to force these people to eat or drink against their will or place a feeding tube. These actions will only cause complications and create suffering. In matters of nutrition and hydration, the compassionate care model must guide all our decisions.

Antibiotics are another complicated issue with chronic problems, as we saw with Freddy. Because they have been used heavily over the years, many resistant strains of bacteria have developed, particularly among the elderly. In hospitals and nursing homes, this has become an enormous problem with epidemic proportions. People with chronic conditions typically develop repeated pneumonias and urinary tract infections, which require antibiotics to treat. Often these antibiotics, after long repeated use, become ineffective and have miserable side effects. The resistant strains of bacteria may be passed on to other people. At end of life, treating symptoms arising from a bacterial infection without antibiotics is possible, and, as a result, other people will not be at risk for resistant strains of bacteria.

There is no way to address all the chronic or acute-care dilemmas that may arise, but our guiding principle must always be the compassionate care Jesus taught us. Our primary focus in the here and now is on spiritual healing while we look forward in hope to a day of physical healing yet to come. When people focus exclusively on cure and prolonging their lives, they may be falling into the trap of idolatry. At this point, we need to curtail or stop the pursuit of curative treatment. If a medical or surgical treatment is immoral and, therefore, unethical, then we must stop the treatment right away. The standards of Scripture are radically different from those of modern medicine, and Christians must be aware of these differences if they are to make biblically informed medical decisions that honor Christ.

Biblically Informed Medical Directives

Finally, it is also consistent with the compassionate health-care model for us to do everything in our power to eliminate undue stress on others through biblically informed health-care planning (Gal. 6:2; 2 Thess. 3:8). Unless we carefully plan and express our health-care wishes in writing and in the appropriate legal format, our desires concerning medical treatment will be unknown. As a result, we may not honor God, health-care professionals will lack guidance, and those close to us may regret the decisions they will have to make. To avoid these consequences, we should prepare biblically informed advance medical directives while we are healthy and possess a sound mind.

An advance medical directive refers to written instructions expressing wishes about future medical care in the event we are unable to speak for ourselves. We formalize our desires in a document called a living will, and we may appoint someone in writing to implement these decisions, a person called a health-care surrogate. If we cannot speak for ourselves, the health-care surrogate will become our voice. It is wise to prepare advance medical directives, but it is even more important to appoint a health-care surrogate with the ability to implement these difficult medical and biblical decisions. A spouse is not necessarily the best choice.

Most standardized living wills assume a monistic approach to the human person and recognize the UDDA, so it is important for people to clarify their wishes on these documents. For example, the form in Florida says, "If my attending or treating physician and another consulting physician have determined that there is *no reasonable medical probability of my recovery* from such a condition" (emphasis mine), then withdraw or withhold life support. The italicized statement refers to the opinion of doctors, gathered from diagnostic equipment. Therefore, it is important to draft a living will that respects a dualistic approach to the human person and conveys a biblical understanding of life and death. Most living wills also have a section for specific instructions, and this is the area to fill out. Below are some suggested clarifying statements.

> In the event I suffer from a cardiac or respiratory arrest and am resuscitated and connected to life support (that is, technology that keeps my heart pumping and lungs breathing) and am diagnosed as being brain-dead or in a persistent vegetative state, I request that I be made comfortable, the life support withdrawn, and that I not be resuscitated.
>
> If life support is withdrawn and my heart and lungs function independently of it but I remain in a brain-dead or persistent vegetative state (or I am diagnosed in the future as being in some other state, such as dementia, in which I cannot make decisions for myself), and if it will not cause complications,

create further suffering, or prolong imminent death, I request that I be given nutritional sustenance and hydration (whether artificial or not) via my gastro-intestinal system only. I do not desire intravenous nutrition or hydration.

If I continue in this unresponsive state (or other terminal state in which I cannot make decisions for myself) and develop any future conditions that may require cardiac resuscitation, mechanical ventilation, shots or infusions of any sort (except to control pain), surgeries, diagnostic tests of any sort (lab draws, urinalysis, X-rays, etc.), dialysis, or antibiotics administered in any way, I refuse them all.

I direct all my treatment to be limited to measures that will keep me comfortable. I expect my treating physician to contact my health-care surrogate prior to any changes in treatment or new medications.

I also understand that if I have a feeding tube, as my bodily condition deteriorates, nutritional sustenance and hydration may cause complications, and at this time my feeding may need to stop.

Also, on most standardized living wills is an area to indicate a person's desire concerning anatomical gifts, or the donation of organs. I already commented on the major difficulty with organ donation. I noted previously that a true declaration of death cannot be made while a person is still on life support. Harvesting organs from brain-dead people with a beating heart still on life support may kill them, which is murder. I have been present at several vent weans (breathing machine is gradually withdrawn) for so-called brain-dead people, and most of these people do not stop breathing right away, nor do their hearts stop beating. Christians need to be extremely careful in this area.

Nevertheless, there is biblical warrant for making anatomical gifts in certain situations. An example of this would be donating a kidney to someone in need. Jesus taught us, "Greater love has no one than this, than to lay down one's life for his friends" (John 15:13). Donating a kidney is an example of self-sacrifice to help alleviate another person's suffering, and it may give a non-Christian the opportunity to experience saving faith in Jesus Christ before he dies. After the transplantation procedure, the reasonable expectation is both the donor and recipient will continue to live.

Being an organ donor on the United States registry is another issue altogether because of the UDDA. Years ago, I was an organ donor, but due to the unethical nature of brain-death criteria, I removed my name from the registry. Although I do not have "organ donor" printed on my driver's license today, on my living will I indicate my desire concerning organ donation, and my wife (who is my health-care surrogate) knows my wishes. I still believe it is permissible to donate my organs, provided the doctors do not pronounce me legally dead while my heart continues to pump. Therefore, I suggest the following statement for organ donation:

> If the life-support apparatus is withdrawn and my heart and lungs cease to function for a period of three minutes, I will consider myself dead. After I am dead, I desire that my organs be preserved any way possible, and I hereby will them to anyone

in need of them. The person receiving my organs needs to know that I donated them to him or her as a gift, with the intent and hope that he or she will repent and believe in Jesus Christ, by God's grace, and that he or she will dedicate his or her life to the advancement of Jesus' kingdom.

Destruction occurs to most body organs if they do not receive blood for a period of five minutes. If a person has not taken a breath and the heart has not had a beat in three minutes, he or she is dead. This stipulation allows death to occur, permits a chance at organ procurement, and serves as a last effort for evangelism.

Due to technological advances in medical science and the underpinnings of modern medicine, we need to be proactive in planning. Completing advance medical directives, such as a living will, will assure us of biblically oriented medical care when we are incapacitated, and it will relieve the stress of decision making for other people. Therefore, it is important for us to make sure the medical care we receive is biblically informed, and not founded on ideologies militating against the compassionate health-care model, the spiritual healing Jesus provides us in the present, and the physical healing He promises in the future. As we attempt to navigate the complex world of modern medical science in the midst of illness, disease, and dying, we need to remember that we rest ultimately in the arms of a loving God who hears and answers our prayers—a topic we will consider next.

Chapter 4

God's Medicine:
Prayer in the Spirit

Chapter 1 explained that God planned everything before time began and that He is in control of all things in time. In light of this fundamental truth of the Christian faith, some may wonder why we should pray. What effect could our prayers possibly have if God has established His unchanging plan for what will happen in our lives? In this chapter, we will consider this important paradox in light of the book of Job and seek to develop a theology for prayer in the midst of illness, disease, and death.

The popular conception of prayer is that we ask and receive, or, in the context of illness, disease, and death, we pray for healing, a variation of asking and receiving. Although this is a part of prayer, it is really a morsel in the Christian life. At its core, prayer is a communal activity with the triune God under the influence of the Holy Spirit (Rom. 8:26–27). The Holy Spirit is communing within us, inspiring us to remember the Father's promises in Christ, moving us to understand His will in light of these promises and our present situation, and enabling us to make requests according to His will in our lives. Through the exercise of prayer, the Spirit leads us into the heavenly recesses of communion with the triune God and His redemptive purposes in the midst of our present circumstances. Prayer is so much more than asking and receiving; it includes reflecting, remembering, thanking, discerning, dialoguing, fellowshipping, groaning, complaining, interceding, depending, meditating, and desiring those things the triune God wants us to have at present, in light of His redemptive purposes.

Suffering Job and Prayerful Communion

Job gives an excellent example of what this type of prayer looks like in action. In the beginning chapters of the book with his name, we encounter an incredible narrative that invites us into God's heavenly court. In the opening scene, we read of angelic creatures passing before God's throne like courtiers, and Satan is among them (1:6). God stops Satan and asks him where he has come from. Satan replies, "From going to and fro on the earth" (1:7). After this inquiry, an important dialogue between God and Satan follows, setting the background for the rest of the book and Job's prayerful struggles.

The dialogue begins as God comments about Job's faithfulness. "Have you considered My servant Job," says God, "that there is none like him on the earth, a blameless and upright man, one who fears God and shuns evil?" (1:8). Satan says that Job serves God only because He has blessed him, but if God took away his blessings, Job would curse Him.

God permits Satan to tempt Job, with the exception that Satan must "not lay a hand on his person" (1:12). Satan departs from God's presence and attempts to draw

Job away from Him. He wreaks havoc on Job's life. First, he instigates a group of neighbors, and they rise up and kill Job's servants (1:15). Next, he conjures a storm to destroy Job's flocks and shepherds (1:16). Then, Satan motivates another group of neighbors to steal his camels and murder their keepers (1:17). Finally, the destroyer uses the weather again. This time a strong wind rises, and its force destroys the home of Job's son and kills all of Job's children inside (1:18–19). Job's world comes quickly crashing down, yet, "in all this Job did not sin nor charge God with wrong" (1:22; 2:10). Defeated, Satan returns to God and accuses Job by saying that he would curse God if he were to suffer physically, which leads to the second challenge for Job. God tells Satan, "Behold, he is in your hand, but spare his life" (2:3–6).

God allows Satan to inflict physical suffering to the point of death. Job develops festering sores all over his body that dry into itchy scabs that peel from his skin (7:5; 30:28, 30). He suffers from fevers, unrelenting pain, and nightmares (7:19; 19:17; 30:17, 30). He becomes anorexic, emaciated, and disfigured. As a result, he looks ghastly, pale, and hideous (2:12; 17:7; 19:19–20). If this were not bad enough, Satan prompts Job's wife and friends, and they increase his mental and spiritual anguish. Satan's fiendish power is unleashed on Job, yet he does not turn away from God. The rest of the book, however, is clear: Job has a profound struggle as he seeks to make sense of his affliction in light of God's promises, redemptive purposes, and will for his life.

Beginning in chapter 3, a series of speeches occurs between Job and his four companions: Eliphaz, Bildad,

Zophar, and Elihu. The dedicated friends sit in silence for seven days staring at Job's grisly appearance. Then, in chapter 3, Job breaks the long, uncomfortable stillness by cursing the day he was born. Job's friends are shocked and at first somewhat sympathetic, but as they interact with Job, they become increasingly accusatory. Job's companions conclude that he has sinned against God and is trying to hide it, and because of this God is punishing him (cf. 4:1–9).

Job feels completely alone. Amid the physical, social, emotional, and spiritual turmoil, the thing that hurts Job most is what appears to be God's anger toward him. Job has experienced difficult times in the past (29:3), but God was always by his side. Now it seems like even God has turned His back on him, and the estrangement is more than he is able to bear.

Job 29:1–6 expresses Job's longing:

> "Oh, that I were as in months past,
> As in the days when God watched over me;
> When His lamp shone upon my head,
> And when by His light I walked through darkness;
> Just as I was in the days of my prime,
> When the friendly counsel of God was over my tent;
> When the Almighty was yet with me,
> When my children were around me;
> When my steps were bathed with cream,
> And the rock poured out rivers of oil for me!"

He longs for God's blessing and favor. His physical affliction, social turmoil, and emotional stress are secondary to his sense of lost communion with God. Job has had an intimate relationship with God, and we see this in the language of 29:4: "when the friendly counsel of God was over my tent." A literal reading of the Hebrew is "when God's council was by my tent," or "when God was an intimate in my tent." This reminds the reader of Genesis 18, where Abraham, the "friend of God" (James 2:23), met with God in a face-to-face encounter. We see that Job, like Abraham, has had a close relationship with God, his intimate friend. He is struggling primarily with the spiritual component of his suffering; it appears to Job that God is no longer his friend.

Job speaks directly to God in the presence of his companions on at least ten occasions.[1] Job's prayers are bold and daring, and some of the things he says to God are shocking to his friends. Job's friends believe that not only is he suffering from some hidden sin in his life, but also he is being punished for his irreverent attitude (cf. 11:1–3).

In chapter 6:8–10, Job reveals the desire of his heart. He is afraid he will not be faithful to God because the affliction will be too much for him to bear, so he asks God to end his life:

> "Oh, that I might have my request,
> That God would grant me the thing that I long for!
> That it would please God to crush me,
> That He would loose His hand and cut me off!
> Then I would still have comfort;
> Though in anguish, I would exult,
> He will not spare;
> For I have not concealed the words of the Holy One."

---

1. These occasions are in 7:7–21; 9:28–31; 10:2–22; 13:20–14:6; 14:13–22; 16:7–8; 17:3–4; 30:20–23; 40:3–5; 42:1–6.

Job wants God to kill him so that he will have the joy of knowing he was faithful to God while he lived. The *New International Version* translates verse 10 with clarity: "Then I would still have this consolation—my joy in unrelenting pain—that I had not denied the words of the Holy One." In his *Introduction to Wisdom Literature,* Derek Kidner catches the essence of Job's attitude when he writes, "The deeper Job's darkness, the more his grip tightens on what he has always stood for, and the more doggedly he gropes for the way home." Behind Job's prayers is a heart of faithfulness to God, his friend, and a desire to follow His sovereign will at all costs.

Job's Prayers in Affliction
In the midst of affliction, Job came to understand more deeply communion with the triune God, spiritual restoration, and God's promises, will, and redemptive purposes for his life. His prayers put him in contact with these greater purposes in the midst of awful suffering.

"Why Have You Set Me as Your Target?" (7:7–21)
In his first prayer in chapter 7, Job reminds God of his mortality and wants to know why He is so critical of him. Job asks God why He has set His sights on afflicting him, but God is silent. Job feels like God is reducing him to nothingness (v. 21). As the prayer closes, Job fires questions at God in rapid succession:

> "Have I sinned?
> What have I done to You, O watcher of men?
> Why have You set me as Your target,
> So that I am a burden to myself?

> Why then do You not pardon my transgression,
> And take away my iniquity?" (vv. 20–21).

Job's eternal friend is silent.

"I Know That You Will Not Hold Me Innocent" (9:28–31)
The next prayer occurs near the end of chapter 9. In this prayer, Job laments the testimony of sin his suffering betrays (v. 28). He confesses his guilt to God, but as he does so, the Holy Spirit reminds him of his inability to make himself innocent (vv. 29–31). Someone else needs to intercede for Job (vv. 33–34), but before he is able to meditate more deeply on this comforting truth, Satan assaults him. As Job draws near his Redeemer to find peace in the midst of affliction (cf. 19:25), Satan attacks on a weak flank, and soon Job wants to bring God before his own bar of justice.

"My Soul Loathes My Life" (10:1–22)
In this prayer Job grumbles about his life, and in the gall of bitterness he feels justified in giving "free course" to his complaints of ingratitude to God (v. 1). Satan uses Job's self-pity and self-justification to darken his thoughts about God's motives toward him, and his prayer becomes a cross-examination of the Creator:

> "Does it seem good to You that You should oppress,
> That You should despise the work of Your hands,
> And smile on the counsel of the wicked?…
> Your hands have made me and fashioned me,
> An intricate unity;
> Yet You would destroy me.…
> And these things You have hidden in Your heart"
>   (vv. 3, 8, 13).

Job has come to the end of his rope, and Satan rejoices. Job concludes this prayer on a bitter note:

> "Cease! Leave me alone, that I may take a little comfort,
> Before I go to the place from which I shall not return,
> To the land of darkness and the shadow of death,
> A land as dark as darkness itself,
> As the shadow of death, without any order,
> Where even the light is like darkness" (vv. 20–22).

"Make Me Know My Transgression" (13:20–14:22)

In chapters 13 and 14 Job prays again, and the work of the Holy Spirit is evident. In his last encounter, Job questioned God's motives toward him, accused God of acting in malevolent ways, and told God he wanted to be left alone. But in this passage, Satan meets defeat once again! Job cannot leave God alone, and he recognizes his utter dependence on Him. In this prayer, Job makes two humble requests: (1) he asks God to stop afflicting him (13:21); and (2) he asks God to communicate with him (13:22). God will answer both of these petitions at the end of the book, but presently Job will have to continue underneath God's afflicting providence and silent posture. In chapter 14, Job prays, "Oh, that You would hide me in the grave, that You would conceal me until Your wrath is past" (v. 13). If God is not willing to remove Job's affliction and communicate with him in the present, then maybe He will be willing to hide him in the grave until His wrath is past.

In this remarkable prayer, Job introduces another new concept: the hope of a bodily resurrection and vindication of his innocence at the end of the age. In this prayer with long-range prophetic significance, Job asks

God to end his life in the present and raise him from the dead on the last day. "God," he prays, "appoint me a set time, and remember me! If a man dies, shall he live again?" (vv. 13–14). The question is rhetorical: yes, he will live again (cf. 19:25–29). "You shall call, and I will answer You" (v. 15). Job, like the rest of the creation, will fall apart, crumble, wear out, age, and experience pain, sorrow, and misery (vv. 18–22). Relief for him may not come in this life, but it will definitely come on the last day. Amazingly, Job anticipates a full vindication of his innocence on judgment day. God does not watch over Job's sin; He has sealed up his transgressions in a bag, and He covers his iniquity (vv. 16–17).

"You Have Shriveled Me Up" (16:7–8; 17:3–4)
Job prays two more times before the book climaxes in the prophetic revelation of the Redeemer. The prayers occur in chapters 16 and 17, and they depict a spiritually broken, emotionally drained, and physically wrecked man longing for restoration with God, his friend. In 16:7–8 Job prays:

> "You have made desolate all my company.
> You have shriveled me up,
> And it is a witness against me;
> My leanness rises up against me
> And bears witness to my face."

In his commentary on Job, Franz Delitzsch translates 17:3–4 as follows:

> Lay down now, be bondsman for me with Thyself;
> Who else should furnish surety to me?!
> For Thou hast closed their heart from understanding,
> Therefore wilt Thou not give authority to them.

This translation communicates ancient legal concepts in a manner modern readers can more easily understand. We see that Job asks God to offer Himself as surety, and we also see God's sovereign prerogative to harden the hearts of people to accomplish His redemptive purposes. God is the one who literally "hides," as in pulling a curtain to conceal something, "the right understanding of the matter," writes Delitzsch. Job's friends can do nothing to help him. Not only has God alienated Job from his friends (16:7–8), but He has also blinded them to Job's actual state of innocence and rendered them powerless to help (17:4).

In ancient Israel, being surety for someone meant to assume responsibility for another person's debt or, in this context, to post a bond. Job's friends have treated him as though he were a criminal undergoing punishment, and here Job seeks his refuge in God and asks Him to show his innocence by laying down a pledge for him. Job is asking God to be a bondsman, or surety, on his behalf in order to free him from his condemnation. Job's bond payment was in the person of God Himself as his redeemer. In ancient Israel, the redeemer had the responsibility of rescuing a family member from debt, hardship, or some other type of trouble (Lev. 25:23–55). In this sense, then, Job asks God to pledge Himself as his redeemer. Job bases his plea on the eternal, timeless covenant of redemption of Ephesians 1:3–14 and the Redeemer of God's elect, the Lord Jesus Christ. "In Him we have redemption through His blood," writes Paul, "the forgiveness of sins, according to the riches of His grace...being predestined according to the purpose of Him who works all things according to the counsel of His will" (Eph. 1:7, 11). Therefore, even in the midst of his deepest pain, depression, and suffering, Job finds assurance and exclaims:

> "I know that my Redeemer lives,
> And He shall stand at last on the earth;
> And after my skin is destroyed, this I know,
> That in my flesh I shall see God,
> Whom I shall see for myself,
> And my eyes shall behold, and not another.
> How my heart yearns within me!" (19:25–27).

Job remembers his spiritual healing, the day of the Lord's favor, which he experienced through types and shadows pointing forward to the incarnation of Christ (his justification), and he looks forward in hope to the day of vengeance of our God, to the day of physical healing at the second coming of Christ when his redemption will be complete (his glorification). Job knows his Redeemer lives, and he knows that he will stand in a glorified resurrection body with Him!

The entire ordeal starts to make sense to Job, and now he sees his suffering in its proper eternal and redemptive context. At this point, God answers Job's earlier requests to remove His afflicting hand and speak to him (see 13:21–22; cf. also 1 John 5:14). In chapters 38 to 41 God fires several questions at Job to teach him that He is the one who asks the questions:

> "Now prepare yourself like a man;
> I will question you, and you shall answer Me.
> Where were you when I laid the foundations of
>   the earth?
> Tell Me, if you have understanding.
> Who determined its measurements?

Surely you know!
Or who stretched the line upon it?
To what were its foundations fastened?
Or who laid its cornerstone,
When the morning stars sang together,
And all the sons of God shouted for joy?" (38:3–7).

Job and God are friends, but they do not stand on equal ground. God condescends to be intimate with us, but He is infinitely holier than we are. God is the eternal, sovereign, wise, providential, and perfect Creator with unquestionable actions. God's purposes will always serve the best interests of His people (Rom. 8:28). Now Job has a better understanding, and he prays,

"Behold, I am vile;
What shall I answer You?...
I have heard of You by the hearing of the ear,
But now my eye sees You.
Therefore I abhor myself,
And repent in dust and ashes" (40:4; 42:5–6).

In Romans 8:28 Paul wrote, "And we know that all things work together for good to those who love God, to those who are the called according to His purpose." God called Job for a purpose, and He calls you and me for the same purpose. We are to live according to God's redemptive purposes, and our prayers need to reflect this reality. Few of us will ever experience extensive losses like Job. He suffered physically, mentally, socially, economically, and spiritually; he was dropped head first into the furnace of affliction, and he did nothing to cause these things to happen (cf. John 9:3)! It was in the midst of affliction, however, that Job understood more deeply communion with the triune God and spiritual restoration. He gained a clearer understanding of God's promises, will, and redemptive purposes for his life, and through our own affliction, we will too. Through his prayers, Job recognized these greater purposes in the midst of awful suffering, and this is what our prayers should accomplish as we face illness, disease, and death today.

Praying in the Midst of Illness, Disease, and Death

Our concept of prayer is often limited to asking and receiving; thus, we tend to focus on asking for healing when we pray regarding sickness. Sometimes Christians assume God wants them to experience physical healing in this life, so they pray to this end. One problem with this assumption is that it misunderstands what Jesus came to do during His incarnate ministry and what He has yet to do at His second coming, a topic we looked at in chapter 1. While it is not wrong to pray for physical healing, the focus of our prayers at this point in redemptive history should be on spiritual restoration in Christ and on the promises of physical healing yet to come. This was Job's focus, and it should be ours.

Why We Should Pray

At the beginning of this chapter, I raised the question of why we should pray if God has already planned for everything and if He is going to accomplish His will regardless of what we say. There are at least three reasons we should pray. First, the Bible commands us to pray. Paul tells us to "pray without ceasing" (1 Thess. 5:17). When Jesus taught His disciples to pray, He said "*when* you pray" (Matt. 6:5, emphasis added), demonstrating His expectation that prayer would be ongoing in a believer's life. Second, prayer reminds us of our dependence on God. Jesus told us to ask God that His "will be done" and to request "daily bread" (Matt. 6:10, 11). Finally, prayer is the means God has appointed to allow us to express our desires to Him. Paul tells us to "let [our] requests be made known to God" (Phil. 4:6). We think primarily of this third aspect when we consider prayer, but equally important is remembering our duty to and dependence on God.

The Bible reminds us that we are completely dependent on God in the act of praying itself. When we pray rightly, we do not pray alone; the indwelling Holy Spirit prays with and for us. Paul writes, "For we do not know what we should pray for as we ought, but the Spirit Himself makes intercession for us with groanings which cannot be uttered. Now He who searches the hearts knows what the mind of the Spirit is, because He makes intercession for the saints according to the will of God" (Rom. 8:26–27). The Holy Spirit is at work in us, enabling us to pray, and He is interceding for us according to God's will. True prayer is Spirit-dependent prayer, so when we pray for others or ourselves in the midst of illness, disease, tragedy, or dying, we need to pray in the Holy Spirit.

This means that our prayers must be rooted in Scripture, which is our touchstone for certainty concerning God's will. Holy Scripture teaches us about spiritual, historical, redemptive, ethical, and moral truths. It provides us with promises to comfort and warn us, advice to direct and lead us, and instruction about the triune God who loved and redeemed us. As important as the confidence Scripture provides is its testimony to our subjective experiences by the Holy Spirit. Scripture must be applied to our souls. It is important to express our thoughts, feelings, and desires in prayer, but they must be subservient to Scripture, and the indwelling Spirit helps to keep us from being led astray.

When we are afflicted, our prayers should include the three important areas that Job's did, recognizing the fuller revelation of Scripture we enjoy. First, we need to pray for clear evidence of salvation in Christ, our Redeemer and the rock on which our unshaken faith is fixed. Second, we should pray for the renewal of the inner man, even as the outer man is dying. Our body may be dying and heading to the grave, but we should pray for inward renewal to occur as the Spirit prepares us for a glorious resurrection body on the day of vengeance of our God. Third, we need to pray that the Holy Spirit will equip us to face illness, disease, and death without fear as we believe in the all-sufficient mercy of Christ without doubting, by tightly embracing the end of our faith—the person of Jesus—and by resting in the merits of His righteousness alone for our salvation, just as Job did.

Pray for the Holy Spirit to Strengthen
Our Union to Christ
Our faith unites us to Christ. It is no surprise, then, that the assurance of this salvation may be an area of great battle for the believer faced with illness, disease, and death. Our bodies are sinful and therefore affected by biochemical imbalances that may cause nervousness, excitability, agitation, and lethargy. Our thinking is sinful and therefore plagued with psychological anomalies that give rise to a whole host of inappropriate thoughts,

feelings, and emotions. Our volition is sinful and therefore full of idolatry, immorality, and rebellion toward God. We also face an enemy, Satan, who is seeking to devour us by preying on this deep-rooted depravity. It is not surprising that when affliction strikes, the body and soul become vulnerable, and Satan ramps up his attacks.

The impairments that come because of sickness may cloud our mental clarity and obscure clear evidences of our salvation in Christ. Faith operates in the realm of abstract thought, which pain, anxiety, fear, depression, and neurological and psychological instability can obscure; therefore, we can be hindered in our exercise of faith in the revealed knowledge of Christ. Medications and other medical and surgical means to treat symptoms may help to assist bodily stability and mental clarity, so we should ask God to bless these means, but we should pray, most importantly, for the Holy Spirit to act directly on our souls to confirm clear evidences of our salvation in Christ.

Jesus said, "If anyone desires to come after Me, let him deny himself, and take up his cross, and follow Me" (Matt. 16:24). This mandate is no less authoritative when we are facing illness, disease, or death. We need to pray that we will not make illness, bodily pain and suffering, and the alleviation of them the focus of our devotion. Christ must be the focus, and any medical, pharmaceutical, or surgical intervention should help us direct our attention to Him. We need to pray that self-pity will not consume us. Self-pity is never justified in the Christian life; only acts of self-denial are, and these will help us see Christ more clearly, use medical and surgical treatment more wisely, and enable us to embrace our salvation in Christ much more tightly.

The ultimate enemy is Satan, as we saw with Job. He is the great deceiver, liar, and murderer. Satan is seeking to devour us, and he does so by preying on bodily, mental, and spiritual weaknesses. He is a master at using human depravity and this fallen world to accomplish his ends. Satan's goal is to obscure the evidences of our salvation in Christ so that we will feel forsaken by God or question His authority over our life. Today, Satan still asks believers, "Has God indeed said?" (Gen. 3:1), and when we are suffering from bodily, mental, and spiritual assaults on every side and death is front and center, he will use this question, or some variant of it, like a crowbar to pry us from our reliance on Christ.

In the area of bodily affliction, Satan will attempt to focus our attention on our suffering. Satan may say things such as, "This suffering is useless; put an end to it! You can commit suicide legally in Oregon and Washington. Overmedicate yourself so that nothing matters. What kind of God would allow you to suffer like this?" On the other hand, he might say, "Do you really think you will be free from this bodily suffering after you die? This is it! Heaven is fiction. You have to live for the here and now. Go after one more treatment. There is another research drug to try. Go after it! Live strong! Spend your life savings on that miracle cure in New Mexico. God wants you to be healed at all costs."

In our mental and spiritual life, Satan will attempt to cause doubt and despair. He will say things such as, "My friend, you have reason to be anxious and fearful. You are dying, and everything you believe is utterly false. Jesus, salvation—this is nonsense! Look, my friend, if God really existed, He would never allow you to go through this. Your hope is built on empty promises from an outdated book." On the other hand, he might say, "Hell is a reality, and that is where you are going! Come on, if you really believed in Jesus, you would not fear death. But look at you! You are afraid, depressed, anxious, sick, sinful—and you call yourself a Christian! God will never accept somebody like you; in fact, He hates you!" We need to pray passionately that the Holy Spirit will empower us to see through Satan's smoke screen so that we may see clearly the evidence of our unbreakable union with Christ.

Pray for the Holy Spirit to Renew the Inner Man
Having prayed that we might clearly perceive the evidences for salvation in Christ, we must pray that we may experience renewal in the inward man, even as the outward man dies. Through the new birth, we are free spiritually from bondage to sin, idolatry, Satan, and death. A process of spiritual renewal began in the whole person. Outwardly, our material bodies are "perishing," writes Paul, yet inwardly our immaterial souls are "being renewed day by day," even as the grave draws near (2 Cor. 4:16). Illness, disease, trauma, decay, death, and all the evils of this present world will take their inevitable toll on us, but we can take heart because inwardly the Holy Spirit is renewing us.

It is important to note that the spiritual renewal we experience does not conclude at death, but rather at the second coming of Christ—the day of vengeance of our God. Therefore, we should pray as John did: "Come, Lord Jesus!" (Rev. 22:20). The consummation of redemption is the goal for us, and this will occur when Jesus returns. On that great day, we will possess a body like the resurrected Christ's, and we will be healed physically. Our prayers, like Job's, must reach past the sufferings of the present to the future hope of peace, rest, bliss, complete healing, and glorification. They must not be nearsighted, looking only to death and our disembodied souls entering heaven; rather, they must be farsighted, looking beyond death and the disembodied existence to the end of the world as we know it, the second coming of Christ, the day of redemption, and the reunification and glorification of our bodies and souls. Our prayers span the annals of time to the end of time, and they need to place our present sufferings within their proper eternal context of redemption, physical healing, restoration, and glorification.

Pray for the Holy Spirit to Embolden Our Claim to Christ's Victory

Finally, we are to pray that we will be able to persevere without fear in the face of death. There is a proper fear of death that helps us avoid situations that may harm us, but there is also a slavish fear of death that compels us to recoil from it at all costs. It is against this slavish fear we are to pray. Our supplication is threefold in this regard. First, we pray for the Holy Spirit to grant us greater trust in the all-sufficient mercy of Christ. Second, we pray for the Holy Spirit to enable us to embrace more tightly the end of our faith—namely, the person of Christ. Third, we pray for the Holy Spirit to help us rest in Christ's merits alone for salvation. Ultimately, we pray for the Holy Spirit to empower us to persevere by confessing unflinchingly, "'O Death, where is your sting? O Hades, where is your victory?' The sting of death is sin, and the strength of sin is the law. But thanks be to God, who gives us the victory through our Lord Jesus Christ" (1 Cor. 15:55–57). Jesus gained the victory over death, and this is our confidence as we endure illness, disease, and death, empowered by the Holy Spirit.

Doubts may assail us, so we pray for stronger faith, which is the antidote to doubt. Jesus said to Thomas, who doubted that the Lord rose from the dead, "Blessed are those who have not seen and yet have believed" (John 20:29). The blessed ones, according to Jesus, are those who have not seen Him physically but who see Him spiritually by faith. We pray for a rock-hard trust in the promises declaring Christ's mercy. The mercies of the tri-une God promised in Jesus cast doubt away, and as we are empowered by the Holy Spirit to embrace them, they strengthen our faith in the person of Jesus.

Jesus is a real, living person who feels, loves, and cares. He shows compassion to us (John 1:14), and He is our family member (Rom. 8:15–17) and friend (John 15:14). We need to pray that we will be able to cling to these truths more tightly, but our prayer should not stop there. Jesus is also unique in His person. He is not only a man, but He is also the perfect God-man Christ (1 Tim. 2:5). Therefore, we pray we will be able to hold onto Christ as mediator, who neutralized our death by His death and resurrection (1 Cor. 15:55–57), opened the way to heaven (Heb. 9:24), and is eagerly waiting to receive us on the other side of the grave (Rev. 21:4).

When we are in the throes of illness, disease, and dying, biochemical, neurological, and psychological changes may occur that will cause us to have evil thoughts, harsh words, or ungodly behaviors. Although remorseful and repentant, we may still feel as if we are not good enough to enter into God's presence. Therefore, we need to pray the Holy Spirit will enable us to rest in Christ's impeccable obedience to the law of God on our behalf. Paul never tired of remembering this truth. He wrote, "I have been crucified with Christ; it is no longer I who live, but Christ lives in me; and the life which I now live in the flesh I live by faith in the Son of God, who loved me and gave Himself for me. I do not set aside the grace of God; for if righteousness comes through the law, then Christ died in vain" (Gal. 2:20–21). Jesus holds us securely, even when we sin against Him (2 Tim. 2:13), for He is the one who kept the law for us, promises us forgiveness, and says to us that we "shall never perish" (John 10:28).

Praying for Healing
Having prayed for the Holy Spirit's work in us, we may ask God to add to our days—if He is willing. When I use the phrase *healing prayer,* I am not thinking of miraculous healing, although God may be inclined to perform a miraculous healing, and sometimes they do occur. It is not special healing prayers, anointing with oil, or laying on of hands that causes these miracles, however; rather, it is the predetermined will of God. If healings coincide with prayer, praise God for His will to heal! Today, for the most part, God is pleased to work through the ordinary means of medical science and health-care professionals to provide us with healing. Therefore, we should pray

for God to bless and use these means, and we should not overly concern ourselves with miracles.

We should desire to live on in this life, provided it is the will of God for us to do so and our living on will enable us to proclaim the year of the Lord's favor. There are three considerations when we pray for physical healing. First, we should ask God to heal the injury, illness, or disease we are experiencing by blessing the application of medical, surgical, or pharmaceutical treatments. Next, we should ask the Holy Spirit to help us recover, rehabilitate, or maintain our present state of health with the treatment and renew our physical strength in the process. Finally, we should pray to the Holy Spirit to remind us of God's deliverance from our affliction and to give thanks for it.

Prayer is God's medicine for us in the midst of illness, disease, trauma, tragedy, and dying. It is through the exercise of prayer that we speak God's words back to Him under the inspiration of the Holy Spirit and enter into the depths of communion with Him like Job. He, in turn, brings comfort, hope, guidance, assurance, and spiritual healing to our souls. Prayer is so much more than asking God for physical healing. It is a spiritual act of worship and communal activity with the Father, Son, and Holy Spirit, where we recognize our utter dependence upon the triune God, His indwelling Spirit, His will, and His redemptive and restorative purposes for our lives. Prayer in the midst of dying keeps our hopes centered on Jesus, and, in light of the hopeless answers modern medicine offers at end of life, this is crucial—a topic we will consider next.

Chapter 5

Hospice Butterflies

In the 1980s, Medicare included a hospice benefit for Americans age sixty-five and older with a terminal diagnosis and prognosis of six months or less to live. Since then hospice care has become an integral part of America's specialized health-care system. Hospice agencies use an interdisciplinary health-care team approach to providing care, and they seek to integrate the professional care and assistance they provide into a patient's living situation. Hospice does not take over caring for a patient and family, but it assists caregivers by providing palliative medical assistance in the context of a patient's family and community. Nurses are the cornerstone of the hospice team, but a medical doctor and social worker are involved in a patient's care as well. These are the core team members Medicare requires for each patient enrolled in a hospice program. Home health aides, chaplains, and volunteers are optional services for patients and families, but Medicare requires they be offered. Most hospices deliver their care in patients' homes, but some hospices have inpatient units to manage difficult end-of-life issues and symptoms.

The goal of hospice care is not to cure a disease but to reduce its symptoms by providing physical, emotional, and spiritual support and care to the patient and family in order to prepare them for death. Hospice care is compassion focused, palliative in nature, and holistic in approach. It reflects the type of care the Good Samaritan gave to the injured man on the side of the road, so this type of care is consistent with Jesus' compassionate care model. The National Hospice and Palliative Care Organization (NHPCO), the group that sets the standards for hospices in the United States, defines hospice care this way:

> Hospice provides support and care for persons in the last phases of an incurable disease so that they may live as fully and as comfortably as possible. Hospice recognizes that the dying process is a part of the normal process of living and focuses on enhancing the quality of remaining life. Hospice affirms life and neither hastens nor postpones death. Hospice exists in the hope and belief that through appropriate care, and the promotion of a caring community sensitive to their needs, that individuals and their families may be free to attain a degree of satisfaction in preparation for death. Hospice recognizes that human growth and development can be a lifelong process. Hospice seeks to preserve and promote the inherent potential for growth within individuals and families during the last phase of life. Hospice offers palliative care for all individuals and their families without regard to age, gender, nationality, race, creed, sexual orientation, disability, diagnosis, availability of a primary caregiver, or ability to pay.

With the exception of a few phrases that allude to the theory of evolution (i.e., "dying process," "normal process of living," "human growth and development," "potential for growth"), this statement reflects a biblical approach to medical care. It is important to note, however, that a person who enters a hospice program desires palliative treatment that is oriented toward comfort, and he is making a decision to allow death to arrive without further curative intervention to prolong life.

A figure who looms large in the movement is the late Dr. Elisabeth Kübler-Ross (1926–2004). In 1969, she published *On Death and Dying,* an indictment of the medical community for its insensitive approach to patients facing death. Kübler-Ross wrote this book before the creation of the PSDA at a time when patients had little to say about their medical care. Also during this time, increasing optimism surrounded the achievements of modern medical science, and the creation of Medicare in 1965 provided health-care institutions millions of tax dollars to tap into for reimbursements. *On Death and Dying* forced the overly optimistic and now lucrative world of medicine to acknowledge again the reality of death, and it exposed the medical community's failure to treat the physical, mental, social, and spiritual components of suffering that accompany it. Kübler-Ross's work effected a positive turning point in modern medicine, but a negative trend arose from another less popular, but no less influential book she wrote called *Death: The Final Stage of Growth.*

In *Death: The Final Stage of Growth,* Kübler-Ross presents death as a transition to a new stage of life, which is similar to beliefs found in Buddhism and Hinduism.

Death, according to Kübler-Ross, ultimately leads to a hereafter in harmony with a person's personal beliefs, whatever those beliefs may be. According to Kübler-Ross, death is the pinnacle event on an evolutionary trajectory of growth and development in the human life cycle. She writes in the preface to the book, "I hope to convey one important message to my readers: namely, that death does not have to be a catastrophic, destructive thing; indeed, it can be viewed as one of the most constructive, positive, and creative elements of culture and life." Kübler-Ross's positive vision concerning death and her pluralistic views about the hereafter reflect the majority consensus of most hospices today in the United States, and this aspect of hospice care is negative.

In keeping with Kübler-Ross's views, the accrediting agency for hospices nationwide, the NHPCO, presents death as a transition point in life similar to the natural process of birth. The following is from the NHPCO's mission statement: "Hospice believes that death is an integral part of the life cycle.... Hospice also recognizes the potential for growth that often exists within the dying experience for the individual and his/her family and seeks to protect and nurture this potential."

For hospice, death is an "integral part" of the "life cycle." Death and birth are similar—a natural part of the circle of life; therefore, the dying person and his family should welcome it and embrace the opportunities for growth it offers. Labor and delivery is a bittersweet experience, and so is death, but the end result in both is precious—a new baby in birth and a transition to a new stage of personalized existence or nonexistence in death.

Before birth, a baby lives in another world and is oblivious to what is outside, and this is how it is for the person who dies, at least according to the contemporary view of death in most hospices throughout the United States.

I do not want to trivialize death or the important end-of-life care hospices provide, but I do want to draw attention to the error of recasting death as a normal part of growth and development in the human life cycle. In birth, painful labor and delivery start, and there is no stopping it, but medications and specialized medical personnel help palliate the symptoms. Suddenly, in birth, the infant leaves one state of existence to enter another, just like the dying person enters a new existence (or nonexistence) through the painful labor of dying. The hospice team, just like the labor and delivery team, is at the dying person's side to palliate symptoms, provide counsel, and give guidance. Just as a mother focuses on the excitement of labor, delivery, and the anticipation of a new baby, so the dying person should focus on death and the potential for growth it offers, anticipating the new phase that is to come.

The hospice movement uses the winsome picture of a butterfly emerging from its cocoon, like a baby from a womb or a soul from its body, and fluttering off into a mysterious new existence to depict death in a pleasant light. The butterfly is one of the hospice movement's icons. In Florida, car owners can purchase a beautifully designed orange and white license plate from the Department of Motor Vehicles with a monarch butterfly on it that says "HOSPICE: Every Day Is a Gift." The butterfly symbolizes a transition from death to this new stage of existence, which is up to you! After a dying person breaks out of the ugly, dry, brownish cocoon of his body, a beautiful butterfly emerges, and it flutters off into a self-customized hereafter. This is the message of the license plate. NHPCO's and hospice's recasting of death is a tragedy because it creates a barrier to the message of the exclusive hope embodied in the year of the Lord's favor.

A Tragic Solution to Suffering

Equally troubling is the rise of voluntary euthanasia or physician-assisted suicide (PAS) to ameliorate suffering, which is law in two states. In 1997, Oregon passed the Death with Dignity Act, granting doctors the legal right to prescribe lethal doses of medications to terminally ill patients so they can commit suicide. Washington followed suit in 2008, passing the Physician Assisted Death Bill, and in 2012 Massachusetts had PAS on the ballot (thankfully, it was voted down). In Montana, a trial court ruled that voluntary euthanasia is legal, and, presently, there is ongoing debate in New Hampshire and California over the issue. Hundreds of people have committed suicide with the help of these laws. Nonvoluntary euthanasia is still a crime in the United States, and in 1999 the NHPCO took a position against voluntary euthanasia. Nevertheless, with NHPCO's depiction of death as a pleasant experience, the government's inability to fund Medicare, and Obamacare's greater control over the health-care industry, we are on a slippery slope regarding euthanasia.

The pain and suffering some people experience from a terminal disease can be awful and even unbearable, but suicide is not the answer. Jesus is the answer, along with aggressive pain and symptom management for suffering. The hospice movement, with its focus on compassionate health care, is a move in the right direction for modern medicine, but its trivialization of death and its agnostic view of the hereafter is tragic. Death is not a state of enlightened growth in an evolutionary process or a transition to a self-customized hereafter. Death is payment for sin: "The wages of sin is death" (Rom. 6:23). Death is not a normal or natural process like birth; rather, it is entirely abnormal and unnatural (Gen. 3:19). God did not originally create us to die. Death is a testimonial to the destructiveness of sin in God's creation (Rom. 8:18–21). It is ugly, awful, and miserable, and suicide is not a solution to the pain and suffering it causes.

Hospices are correct in seeing death as a transition from one state of existence to another. For the believer, it is a transition to everlasting bliss (Rev. 21:4), but for the unbeliever it is a move from one state of suffering to another—one intensified beyond comprehension. If a person does not embrace the year of the Lord's favor while he is living, he will enter into a state of everlasting agony, misery, hopelessness, and anguish after this life (Rev. 21:8). The resurrection of Christ is the *only* answer to death, providing us with the only assurance for a positive transition to true life, healing, and human wholeness that never ends. In reality, the butterflies of hospice are not innocent icons of comfort in the face of death and suffering; rather, they are a fluttering cloud of moths obscuring the true light of Christ and His resurrection.

The Only Hope in Death: The Resurrection of Jesus

In 1 Corinthians 15 Paul writes about the resurrection of Christ and His exclusive victory over sin, suffering, and death. Paul begins this chapter by proving the historical reality of Christ's resurrection (vv. 1–11), and he moves on to explain how central it is to the message of the gospel (vv. 12–19). According to Paul, the Christian faith is meaningless without the literal resurrection of Jesus (vv. 29–41). "If Christ is not risen," writes Paul, "your faith is futile; you are still in your sins!" (v. 17). Next, Paul gives his readers information about the future, including the return of Jesus Christ, the day of vengeance of our God, and our own mysterious bodily resurrection at His second coming (vv. 20–28, 42–44). Paul concludes the chapter proclaiming Jesus' resurrection victory over sin, sickness, suffering, and death (vv. 55–57), and he moves on to exhort believers to stand firm against false beliefs, with unflinching confidence in the resurrection of Christ from the dead (v. 58).

Paul is persistent in his effort to prove the literal resurrection of Christ, because there were scoffers in his day (cf. Acts 17), just as in our own. The fact that Jesus rose from the dead is of primary importance for Christians, and Paul wants to drive this truth home. Paul writes:

> For I delivered to you first of all that which I also received: that Christ died for our sins according to the Scriptures, and that He was buried, and that He rose again the third day according to the Scriptures, and that He was seen by Cephas, then by the twelve. After that He was seen by over five hundred brethren at once, of whom the greater part remain

to the present, but some have fallen asleep. After that He was seen by James, then by all the apostles (1 Cor. 15:3–7).

The resurrection did not occur in an obscure corner, as Paul points out in his trial before Agrippa and Felix (Acts 26). The Old Testament prophets predicted the resurrection of Christ hundreds of years before it happened, and Jesus referred to it repeatedly when He walked on the earth. There was eyewitness testimony as well. After His resurrection, Jesus was seen by Mary, Peter, John, the other apostles, more than five hundred people, and James (1 Cor. 15:5–8). Paul is emphatic in his desire to prove Christ's resurrection as a historic fact, because without it, the Christian faith is meaningless.

Paul's line of reasoning does not stop there, however. Some in Corinth affirmed the resurrection of Christ but were skeptical about a future bodily resurrection. In a rather intricate argument, Paul uses their skepticism about a future bodily resurrection to bolster his defense for Christ's bodily resurrection. Paul reasons thus:

Now if Christ is preached that He has been raised from the dead, how do some among you say that there is no resurrection of the dead? But if there is no resurrection of the dead, then Christ is not risen. And if Christ is not risen, then our preaching is empty and your faith is also empty. Yes, and we are found false witnesses of God, because we have testified of God that He raised up Christ, whom He did not raise up—if in fact the dead do not rise. For if the dead do not rise, then Christ is not risen. And if Christ is not risen, your faith is futile; you are still in your sins! Then also those who have fallen asleep in Christ have perished. If in this life only we have hope in Christ, we are of all men the most pitiable (1 Cor. 15:12–19).

Paul's logic is clear. If there is no future bodily resurrection, then there is no resurrection at all, and if this is the case, Jesus has not risen from the dead. Jesus is still in the grave, sin and death still have us in their grip, the preaching of the life-giving gospel is meaningless—even deceitful—and the Christian life is a farce. People would be better off embracing the agnosticism of hospice agencies and holding on tight to the science of hope to live on at all costs. Thank God, this is not the case!

The fact is, Paul asserts, "Christ is risen from the dead" (1 Cor. 15:20). Paul uses the phrase translated "is risen" and its various forms seven times in this chapter, and they are translated from a single Greek verb in the perfect tense that indicates Christ's resurrection was a completed act in time. At the beginning of 1 Corinthians, Paul focused on the undisputed fact of the suffering and death of Christ on the cross (1:23; 2:2), and at the end of the letter he focuses on the reality of Jesus' resurrection. The central message of the Christian faith is the historic suffering, death, burial, and resurrection of Jesus Christ as a completed act in time. This is the message of the year of the Lord's favor, the objective testimony we look to with faith and hope, and it is the *only* answer to illness, disease, and death in the world today, but it is being obscured by the religious pluralism and agnosticism endorsed by the hospice movement and modern medicine.

Hell Is Real

The writer to Hebrews says, "It is appointed for men to die once, and after this the judgment" (Heb. 9:27). Death is a terrible reality, but what happens after death is even worse for those who do not believe in the resurrection of Christ. The ultimate tragedy of voluntary euthanasia and hospice butterflies is they deny the reality of an absolute Judge who sentences guilty sinners to an eternal place called hell after they die. Even more tragic than this, however, are influential authors like Rob Bell, who wrote the best-selling *Love Wins*, which says unbelievers will experience salvation after death, and the late John Stott, who teaches that unbelievers will cease to exist after they die because God will annihilate them, and the Catholic doctrine of purgatory. These three teachings and their variations do not line up with the Bible. What happens after death is so important to the writers of the Bible that they leave no room for confusion. The words of the apostle Paul ring clear: "[God] 'will render to each one according to his deeds': eternal life to those who by patient continuance in doing good seek for glory, honor, and immortality; but to those who are self-seeking and do not obey the truth, but obey unrighteousness—indignation and wrath" (Rom. 2:6–8).

People's unwillingness to accept at face value what the Bible says about God's judgment and hell confuses this matter. Hell is a real place of wrath reserved for those who are guilty before the judge of the universe, those who chase after the illusive, false hopes Asclepius and modern medicine offer. The Bible teaches this doctrine clearly in the Old and New Testaments.

In Daniel 12:2 the prophet writes, "Many of those who sleep in the dust of the earth shall awake, some to everlasting life, some to shame and everlasting contempt." John the Baptist, the last of the Old Testament prophets, said of Jesus, "His winnowing fan is in His hand, and He will thoroughly clean out His threshing floor, and gather His wheat into the barn; but He will burn up the chaff with unquenchable fire" (Matt. 3:12). Jesus will separate the wheat (believers) from the chaff (unbelievers), and He will burn the chaff "with unquenchable fire," that is, unrelenting torment. In Mark 9, Jesus tells His disciples that it is better for them to cut off a sinful hand and pluck out an eye that causes them to sin and go through life maimed than to continue sinning with two hands and eyes and "go to hell, into the fire that shall never be quenched—where 'Their worm does not die and the fire is not quenched'" (vv. 43–47).

Daniel, John the Baptist, and Jesus leave no doubt about the reality of "everlasting contempt" for unbelievers, and they emphasize their urgent need to repent and embrace the year of the Lord's favor. Hell is real, awful, and forever. The person who truly loves speaks the truth and does not sugarcoat it, deny it, or manipulate it. Jesus loves; therefore, He taught more about conscious torment in a literal place called hell than He did about everlasting bliss in heaven.

The most famous parable Jesus told on the subject of fixed conscious destinies after death was Lazarus and the nameless rich man in Luke 16:19–31. Although this parable does not teach a theology of hell, its main point is a warning to self-assured, self-deceived, selfish people who think only about themselves and refuse to hear the word of God. The nameless rich man in the story did not care for his neighbor, Lazarus, nor did he listen to Moses and the prophets, so he went to the place self-centered and hardened people go after they die—hell.

The experience of the nameless rich man in Hades is significant. He does not enter a state of soul sleep, he is not annihilated, he does not experience universal salvation, and he does not enter a holding station to be purged of sin. The nameless man is conscious of his torment and the blessing Lazarus receives. He looks up and sees Abraham far away, and at his side is Lazarus, the one he despised in life. Jesus is not teaching that people in hell can look into heaven and vice versa; rather, He is making a point of the absolute and final destinies of Lazarus and the nameless rich man, who are both consciously aware of where they reside. Lazarus is in the place of comfort and bliss at Abraham's side that is far away from the rich man's place of misery and torment—a place bereft of the Abrahamic blessings. The rich man's arrogance is apparent, even in hell. He has the audacity to tell Abraham to send Lazarus to save his family, but Abraham replies, "They have Moses and the prophets" (Luke 16:29), and by that he means that they have God's Word, which explains the solution. Hell is the place for those who live for this world, seeking the favor of Asclepius and modern medicine, who ignore the year of the Lord's favor and chase after butterflies by clinging to another teaching rather than embracing the literal, historic resurrection of Jesus Christ.

The decisive finality of hell should shake Christians to the core. Unbelievers *will* experience torment in hell forever. When Jesus walked on the earth, He pointed to a garbage dump just outside the walls of Jerusalem that burned perpetually as a horrid image to depict hell. It was an unholy and disgraceful place of awful memories, where people offered child sacrifices to pagan gods and goddesses. Jesus pointed to an actual location because hell is a real place people go to after death. The year of the Lord's favor has expired in hell, and there is no more hope there for anything different. Hell is a place and perpetual existence of real psychological, spiritual, and bodily pain and misery, as the wrath of God is unleashed on the self-centered and self-deceived person without intermission or remission. Hell is real!

Hospice's butterfly concept of death tones down its utter ugliness, and it is an outright denial of Christ's exclusive answer to suffering and death. The central point of nearly every apostolic sermon was the resurrection of Christ and the hope it provides for victory over sin, the world, Satan, suffering, sickness, death, and hell. The Bible is emphatically clear—people who do not have hope in the historic resurrection of Christ and embrace His teachings have no hope in life or death (Eph. 2:12). There is an urgent need for the church to proclaim boldly that hospice butterflies are deadly, belief in the resurrection of Christ is an absolute necessity, and hell is a real place with conscious suffering.

The Mission of the Church at End of Life
How does the church proclaim the year of the Lord's favor to a dying world chasing after hospice butterflies? Preaching is important, but equally important are local congregations working side by side with community hospice agencies. A grassroots movement would be most

effective. While they promote distorted ideas about death and the hereafter, hospice programs still embrace components of the compassionate care model described in this book. The NHPCO and most local hospices still affirm life. In my experience working at different hospices through the years, I have found that hospice employees, particularly professional clinicians and skilled aides, enter this field because they feel called to do so. Most of them are caring, compassionate, sincere, selfless, and proficient at what they do, whether they are Christians or not. These people, for the most part, recognize the importance of integrating the care they give into a patient's community, and they do not seek to take over. Local congregations can easily work together with these people and programs and in turn may demonstrate through word and deed the year of the Lord's favor and the power of Christ's resurrection hope over against hospice butterflies.

In fact, the Bible commands us to care for one another as we are able, and not to give over these responsibilities to professional organizations. First Corinthians 12 explains that we are members of one body, possessing different gifts and abilities that we must use to serve one another. God instructs us to bear one another's burdens willingly and to enter into each other's experiences of suffering (1 Cor. 12:26; Gal. 6:2). "Above all things," says Peter, we are to "have fervent love for one another," be hospitable to each other, and use the gifts and abilities we have received from God to care for one another (1 Peter 4:8–10). When people are sick and facing death, counseling, mercy, and hospitality needs arise that the church is equipped to address, such as visiting to read the Bible; praying; singing psalms, hymns, and spiritual songs; holding hands; providing breaks for family members; helping with housecleaning and chores; caring for pets; and assisting with financial needs and management. Our willingness to serve one another with our special gifts and abilities in the name of Christ is a powerful testimony to the unifying power of Christ's resurrection. This is proclaiming the year of the Lord's favor in action, but equally important is proclaiming it in word.

Five important teachings in particular are an encouragement to Christians facing death and also a powerful witness to hospice personnel. I suggest we talk openly about these five points when we are visiting with someone who is sick, if we are suffering from an illness, or when people in the community call on us to visit.

1. Speak about the freeness and fullness of God's grace to save sinners. God's grace is an ocean of unfathomable depth that crashes upon the shore of our lives, wave upon wave, and God has been pleased to grant us access to it.

2. Speak about the all-sufficient righteousness of Christ freely applied to us. Jesus paid it all, and nothing more can be added.

3. Speak about the gracious promises of salvation reserved exclusively for Christians. We do not need to fear death and hell any longer. Christ removed the sting of death and the terror and curse of hell for us, but for the unbeliever it remains.

4. Speak about the indissoluble union we have with Christ. Nothing will ever separate us from Christ—not illness, disease, nor even death.

5. Speak about the hope of the bodily resurrection we have in Christ. Jesus will return one day, on the day of vengeance of our God, and redemption, physical healing, and spiritual restoration will be complete.

Most hospice personnel, and even many church-going Christians, know very little about these five fundamental teachings of the Christian faith, so we must proclaim them boldly to all.

Death is no longer an evil that Christians fear, but it should be a terror to the unbeliever. We need to rest comfortably, trusting in Christ's victory over death while at the same time talking about the horror of death for those whose hope is not in Him. We should be radically intolerant of any teaching regarding death that does not have the resurrection of Christ at its center. Death has no power over Christians, and we need to rejoice, boast, and proclaim this truth. Jesus, through His death, destroyed Satan, who possesses the power of death, and He freed us from slavery to death (Heb. 2:14–15). Jesus also removed the sting of death, which is sin (1 Cor. 15:56). Death will not harm us because Jesus deactivated its power, removed its sting, and dethroned its master, but death will infinitely injure the unbeliever because he is still underneath its magnetic force, poisoned by its sting, and ruled by its master.

At the time of our death we are made perfect in holiness (Heb. 12:23), and our souls enter immediately into heaven (2 Cor. 5:1–8). Our bodies remain mysteriously united to Jesus in their resting place (Isa. 57:2), waiting until He returns (Job 19:26–27). When the day of vengeance of our God arrives, our bodies will miraculously reassemble, rise, and be reunited to our souls. We will possess a glorious resurrection body like Jesus' (1 Cor. 15:43). We will enter into the experience of perfect blessedness—with a glorified body and soul to experience true physical healing—in order to participate in the full enjoyment of the triune God for all eternity in a renewed world without sin, Satan, illness, disease, and death!

"In My Father's house are many mansions," said Jesus. "If it were not so, I would have told you. I go to prepare a place for you" (John 14:2). Jesus entered into heaven, where He is at work not only interceding on our behalf but also preparing a place of incomprehensible comfort for us. It is a place where He will dwell with us and "will wipe away every tear from [our] eyes." It is a beautiful place of peaceful bliss; "there shall be no more death, nor sorrow, nor crying. There shall be no more pain, for the former things have passed away" (Rev. 21:3–4). Most importantly, it is a place promised to us and described by Jesus, who is the embodiment of truth. Jesus teaches a radically different doctrine from the one we looked at earlier in this chapter and throughout this book, which is the pluralized and relativized fiction created by Kübler-Ross, endorsed by the NHPCO, and received as authoritative truth by many hospice-care providers and hospitals. The world needs to hear about Jesus' answer to death, dying, and eternity, and it is up to the church to proclaim these doctrines boldly in order to expose and destroy untruths and save people from the myth of Asclepius, the hopelessness of modern medicine, and the infinite torments of hell.

Conclusion

At the beginning of the book I quoted Philippians 1:21, "For to me, to live is Christ, and to die is gain," and suggested we ask ourselves two important questions: (1) Are we living for Christ in the midst of a medical crisis? (2) Do we see our death as great gain as we look in hope to Christ? I trust the preceding chapters were helpful as you reflected on these two important questions. Answering the first question is easier than answering the second, because the first has to do with how we use modern medical science, our goals when we are sick, and how we care for others in the midst of a medical crisis. The second question is not so easy to answer. The thought of our life ending is sobering, whether we are Christians or not. Death is difficult to face, but the way we answer the first question will have a great impact on our answer to the second.

Throughout this book, I have attempted to show the limits of modern medicine and the futility of trusting in it for healing. I have also exposed some of its underlying ideologies and sought to illustrate the tight grip it can have on us. Modern medicine is a philosophical approach to health care; therefore, it is different from medical science, which is empirical in its approach. The assumptions modern medicine makes are theoretical; they are not factual, nor are they verifiable. Therefore, the compassionate health-care model developed in chapter 1 is a viable option for medical science today. It is up to us to apply this model of care derived from Jesus' life and teaching, which means focusing on spiritual healing at present, using medical science biblically, and looking forward in hope to a day of physical healing yet to come. If we do this, we will live for Christ.

We saw that the foundation for true health, wellness, and life is rooted in the triune God's eternal plan of redemption. The entire world is right where God wants it, and everything in our lives will come about just as He has planned. We cannot understand this completely, and mysteries abound, but this is what the Bible teaches, and in light of the options, it makes the most sense. When we embrace this view of life, the result is a firm foundation to rest on no matter what happens to us. When we see our lives under the matrix of redemption, we will live properly and experience true healing. Prayer in the Spirit is God's medicine to help us live properly in the face of illness, disease, and death, so we need to pray continually. When we pray we commune with the Father, Son, Holy Spirit, and other Christians, and the result is a pursuit of true health, wellness, and life in the context of redemption. We need to live out God's redemptive purposes, demonstrate compassion, and proclaim Christ's exclusive victory over illness, disease, and death. Today is the day of the Lord's favor, but the day of vengeance of our God is fast approaching.

I would like to conclude with some practical suggestions for three spheres of Christian life: individual, congregational, and missionary. First, much of this book focused on living as individual Christians. This is where change needs to start. Unless we rethink our approach to modern medicine and seek to apply the compassionate health-care model to our private lives, our goals will not change and our use of health care will be no different from the rest of the people in the United States. The way we understand, approach, and use medical science needs to be rooted in Scripture. We need to develop a clear, biblical worldview for medical science and live it out, and this needs to start with individual Christians.

Second, the local congregation can be a powerful witness to the community as it cares for members who are in the midst of a medical crisis, but the congregation's witness should not stop there. Our congregations should be sanctuaries people look to for compassionate care, spiritual healing, godly ethics, and hope, and the communities we live in should be aware that our congregation offers these things. Our desire to show compassion, however, must never compromise our message. We need to speak boldly about sin, the absolute need to embrace Christ, and the reality of hell. There is an urgent need for local congregations to become bastions of biblical truth people look to for answers concerning health-care issues and places where people can find spiritual healing and true hope.

A local congregation can do several things to serve its community. One is an end-of-life care visitation ministry, but this type of ministry need not be only at end of life. A local congregation may have a visitation ministry to all types of people in any stage of life at hospitals, nursing homes, private homes, and assisted living facilities. If a congregation chooses to implement a ministry like this it is important to make clear that medical care will not be provided (unless the visitor is a health-care worker and care is consented to by both parties), and visitors will openly discuss the doctrines mentioned here. Due to our litigious society, it may be wise to draft an agreement to define clearly these points for participants. Numerous possibilities for a congregational ministry exist, depending on the skills, callings, and gifts of the people in a particular congregation.

A unique ministry for a health-care professional in the congregation may be as a health-care advocate and counselor. Some congregations have a parish nurse to fill this role. This is an excellent idea, provided the person possesses a biblical understanding of medical science. The person serving in this role would do all that a parish nurse would do (preventive medical teaching, physical evaluations, referral source), as well as assist people with difficult medical decisions, draft medical directives, and act as a liaison to the health-care community. This member could also serve as a health-care surrogate (described in chapter 3) and remove this difficult burden from family members. The health-care advocate-counselor must not usurp the pastor's work as a spiritual counselor, however, but must work in tandem with him in this diaconal role.

The seminary-trained pastor is the person called and equipped by God to apply biblical teaching to life and provide pastoral counseling. His training included painstaking biblical exegesis in the original languages, systematic theology, and pastoral counseling, among other disciplines of study. Most of the issues mentioned in this book have little to do with medical science and more to do with a biblical approach to medical science. The pastor understands why we experience illness, disease, tragedy, and death, and he has the prayerful answers, biblical wisdom, and counsel to help people in the midst of medical crises. He may also be a voice that communicates to the community, proclaiming a compassionate health-care program based on the principles Jesus taught us.

Third, a dream of mine is to establish a compassionate health-care mission in the United States, one that would offer a complete rethinking and overhaul of health care in America designed for people who want to keep Jesus and His agenda at the center of their medical care. What a wonderful testimony it would be to the unifying power of Christ and His compassion working through us if churches who share the same core convictions united to advance this compassionate health-care plan across the nation: a nationwide health-care network of medical clinics, hospitals, nursing homes, assisted-living facilities, home health agencies, and hospices, all rooted in a biblical worldview and funded by the church at large! Compassion and hope in Christ would govern a medical care that would be available to all.

How would a program like this work? Each individual seeking care would receive a comprehensive medical assessment, and, based upon the findings, an interdisciplinary medical team (doctor, nurse, social worker, pastor, and any other needed specialty) would gather to develop prayerfully a palliative care plan to treat pain, suffering, and symptoms in light of biblical wisdom, ethics, and God's redemptive plan. Compassionate medical, surgical, and pharmaceutical care with the goal of advancing the gospel would be the focus, not aggressive, curative intervention to prolong life at all costs. Those who desire this compassionate health-care plan based upon Jesus' principles would receive it without cost, but those who want to opt out of it for more aggressive, life-prolonging treatment rooted in the science of hope would be free to do so. United like-minded churches could be a powerful domestic missionary force with a health-care program like this, and they would positively influence the ongoing health-care debacle in Washington. This dream of mine is rooted in the principles derived from the parable of the Good Samaritan and Jesus' life and teaching, only on a much larger scale.

For Further Reading

Compassionate Jesus had as its main focus a consideration of how Christians should think about modern medicine and its underlying principles, and, as we've seen, a number of subjects are relevant to the topic, including biblical doctrine, prayer, philosophy, and medical science. We've been able to touch on these subjects only briefly here, and you may find that further reading will help you as you strive to rethink the Christian approach to modern medicine. The following are some of the best, most accessible books dealing with these interrelated subjects.

Baxter, Richard. *The Saint's Everlasting Rest*. Edited by Benjamin Fawcett. Grand Rapids: Baker, 1978.

This abridged version makes *The Saint's Everlasting Rest* accessible for most readers, while those who enjoy a more challenging read might consider the original. The chapter on "The Saint's Rest Is Not to Be Expected on Earth" is very convicting, while "Heavenly Contemplation" is extremely uplifting.

Beeke, Joel. R. *Living for God's Glory: An Introduction to Calvinism.* Orlando: Reformation Trust, 2008.

This book is an excellent introduction to Calvinism, demonstrating the robust thoroughness of the Reformed faith for all of life.

Beeke, Joel R. and James A. La Belle. *Living by God's Promises.* Grand Rapids: Reformation Heritage Books, 2010.

Many Christians attempt to live by sight when they are supposed to live by faith and hope in God's promises. Beeke and La Belle do an excellent job of recounting the Puritan view of living by the promises of Scripture in all of life.

Beeke, Joel R. and Brian G. Najapfour. *Taking Hold of God: Reformed and Puritan Perspectives on Prayer.* Grand Rapids: Reformation Heritage Books, 2011.

This is the best book I have read on prayer, particularly the chapter "Thomas Boston on Praying to Our Father." Much praying today focuses on making requests, but this book teaches the prayerful reader to commune in prayer with the sovereign and good God of the Bible.

Bennett, Arthur, ed. *The Valley of Vision: A Collection of Puritan Prayers and Devotions.* Edinburgh: Banner of Truth Trust, 2003.

The Valley of Vision is a collection of Puritan prayers compiled and listed by topic. It has been a part of my daily devotional routine for several years. Every time I pray and meditate through it, it warms my heart and deepens my prayer life. The prayers it includes are drawn from Scripture and are inspirational, comforting, and profound. They also serve as a model for those who wish to grow more deeply in their own prayer lives. *The Valley of Vision* should sit next to everyone's Bible.

Berkhof, Louis. *Louis Berhof's Summary of Christian Doctrine.* Yulee, Fla.: Good Samaritan Books, 2012.

This book is a concise version of Berkhof's *Summary of Christian Doctrine.* It was edited to provide the busy lay reader with an overview of the Reformed faith in order to cultivate a sound biblical worldview for all of life.

Bogosh, Christopher. *The Golden Years: Healthy Aging and the Older Adult.* Yulee, Fla.: Good Samaritan Books, 2013.

This book is for caregivers and people over age sixty-five and addresses the problems of this group in the context of a biblical worldview. The book looks at the components of aging, practicing preventive health care, managing health care, common health problems and loss, and chronic health conditions such as dementia. It also has a section on Affordable Care Act's changes to Medicare.

————. *The Puritans on How to Care for the Sick and Dying: A Contemporary Guide for Pastors and Counselors.* Yulee, Fla.: Good Samaritan Books, 2011.

As the title suggests, this book provides advice on how to care for people who are sick and dying based on "Of the Visitation of the Sick" in the Westminster Confession of Faith. The book is organized to help pastors and counselors discern cases of conscience and apply the proper biblical remedy.

Boston, Thomas. *Human Nature in Its Eternal State.* Yulee, Fla.: Good Samaritan Books, 2012.

This book is extracted from Thomas Boston's *Human Nature in Its Fourfold State.* The section on "Human Nature in Its Eternal State" is extremely relevant for our day, and this little book has been published with updated language. Boston addresses death, the difference between the believer and unbeliever in death, the bodily resurrection, final judgment, hell, and heaven from a thoroughly biblical perspective.

Bridges, Jerry. *Trusting God: Even When Life Hurts*. Colorado Springs: NavPress, 1988.

Experiencing a time of adversity in his own life, author Bridges began a lengthy Bible study on God's sovereignty, and in this book he shares the fruit of his study. He reassures his readers of God's concern for them and His control over their lives, encouraging them to know God better. As we know Him better, we trust Him more completely, even when life hurts.

Carson, D. A. *Christ and Culture Revisited*. Grand Rapids: Eerdmans, 2008.

This book provides analysis and critique of Richard Niebuhr's popular book *Christ and Culture*, which has been a standard read for many Christians in the medical field. Carson shows how Niebuhr's views are fundamentally unbiblical and, in the second half of the book, presents Christ and culture from a biblical viewpoint.

―――. *The Gagging of God: Christianity Confronts Pluralism*. Grand Rapids: Zondervan, 1996.

This book is large but well worth the read. Don Carson's research is voluminous, and he brings the reader up-to-date on cultural issues up to 1996 (his other two books included here bring the reader to the present). He shows the effects of pluralism and how it has influenced the thinking of many unwitting Christians. Some professional Christian groups and organizations, in their desire to be united in their professions, have adopted forms of

Christian pluralism that actually compromise fundamental doctrines of the Christian faith.

―――. *The Intolerance of Tolerance.* Grand Rapids: Eerdmans, 2012.

In this book on culture, Carson demonstrates how intolerant the so-called secular idea of tolerance is. The foundation of modern medicine in America is based upon the ideas of pluralism and tolerance; these views are not tolerant at all but are actually agnostic and, therefore, radically antibiblical.

Cooper, John W. *Body, Soul, and Life Everlasting: Biblical Anthropology and the Monism-Dualism Debate.* Grand Rapids: Eerdmans, 1989.

In a day when monism (i.e., we are only a congeries of biochemical substances with no real soul) rules, even among many healthcare workers professing to be Christian, Cooper presents the biblical view of holistic dualism. He steers clear of Platonism and posits a view of the human person that is biblical through and through.

Cosby, Brian H. *Suffering and Sovereignty: John Flavel and the Puritans on Afflictive Providence.* Grand Rapids: Reformation Heritage Books, 2012.

Many Christians believe they have a duty to protect God and His ways by saying He only permits affliction, as if it were outside His control. Focusing on the writings of Puritan John Flavel, who endured great suffering while embracing God's will, this book reminds the reader that God is absolutely sovereign. God does not permit circumstances; He decrees them. "But our God is in heaven; He does whatever He pleases" (Ps. 115:3).

Edwards, Jonathan. *Heaven, a World of Love.* Lindenhurst, N.Y.: Great Christian Books, 2010. Also online at "Heaven, A World of Love." http://www.tabernakel.nl/data/scans-originele-versie/11-01-Origineel.pdf.

This sermon provides a word picture of heaven that lifts the soul. Edwards speaks about the love of the Father, flowing to the Son and Spirit, out to the heavenly angels, to all the elect, filling heaven itself, and eventually flowing to all the earth at the second coming of Christ. Those who need a break from a world filled with misery will find comfort as they meditate on this sermon. "And now abide faith, hope, love, these three; but the greatest of these is love" (1 Cor. 13:13).

Guthrie, Nancy, ed. *O Love That Will Not Let Me Go: Facing Death with Courageous Confidence in God.* Wheaton, Ill.: Crossway, 2010.

Guthrie compiles writings from contemporary and traditional theologians on the topic of death and dying. This book offers wonderful insights. "My Father Taught Me How to Die" by R. C. Sproul was very moving, and "What More Should God Do to Persuade You to Accept Death Willingly" by Martin Luther is extremely practical.

Horton, Michael S. *A Place for Weakness: Preparing Yourself for Suffering.* Grand Rapids: Zondervan, 2006. Previously titled *Too Good to Be True.*

A series of powerful readings that demonstrate that in earthly difficulties, our Father always keeps His promises from Scripture and works all things together for our good. The author addresses today's common misconception that Jesus is a product for promoting health and happiness. Yet Christians become ill, depressed, bankrupt, and face death.

He shows readers how we can follow even these difficult routes by faith.

Miller, Paul. *A Praying Life: Connecting with God in a Distracting World*. Colorado Springs: NavPress, 2009.

A practical, biblical, and very readable book on prayer. The author encourages readers to understand prayer as the "conversation where your life and your God meet." He considers what it means to pray like a child, habits that can dull our hearts to prayer, barriers to asking that come from the spirit of our age, how having a praying life makes us enter into the story God is weaving in our lives, and practical tools and ways of praying. Through a time of suffering, the author says, he learned to pray, and in this book he passes along the lessons he learned.

Pink, A. W. *The Sovereignty of God*. Edinburgh: Banner of Truth Trust, 1998.

This book exists in several editions and has become a classic on the Reformed doctrine of God's sovereignty. I read this book many years ago, and one of the things I most remember is how Pink presents a clear, irrefutable picture of God's sovereignty from the pages of Scripture. I have met many people through the years, who, after reading this book, were convinced of God's absolute sovereign power over His creation and creatures.

Robinson, Daniel. *Consciousness and Its Implications*. Chantilly, Va.: The Teaching Company, 2007.

Dr. Robinson is a Roman Catholic with a doctorate in neuropsychology. In these lectures, Robinson interacts with the mind-body problem. Throughout, he shows the ethical implications of believing we have only a brain and not a real soul or mind. He uses several examples to show the implications of this belief, most notably Karen Quinlan and Terry Schiavo. Robinson's work is enlightening, especially when the presumption exists today that brain death is a legitimate determiner of death.

Teresi, Dick. *The Undead: Organ Harvesting, The Ice Water Test, Beating-Heart Cadavers—How Medicine Is Blurring the Line between Life and Death.* New York: Pantheon Books, 2012.

The author of this book is not a Christian, but he does have legitimate ethical insights about death determination. Teresi is a journalist who writes on scientific topics. In this book, he exposes the awful practice in America of harvesting organs from donors who may not be truly dead.

Wright, N. T. *Surprised by Hope: Rethinking Heaven, Resurrection, and the Mission of the Church.* New York: Harper Collins, 2008.

Although Wright is appropriately criticized in Reformed circles for his views on justification by faith, we must not mistakenly think that all his theology is misinformed; he is excellent on the resurrection hope. Here, the discerning reader will find Wright's thesis to be a necessary remedy for today's church. Many Christians are focused on the here and now, living for the next minute, hour, and day, so that the second coming of Christ and the resurrection hope are all but forgotten. According to Wright, this is not the way the ancient church lived.